HITTING THE AARON WAY

HITTING

THE AARON WAY

WAY

HANK AARON
with Joel Cohen

PRENTICE-HALL, INC., Englewood Cliffs, N.J.

Drawings by Tony Kokinos

Hitting the Aaron Way by Hank Aaron
with Joel Cohen
Copyright © 1974 by Hank Aaron and
Joel Cohen

Prentice-Hall International, Inc. London
Prentice-Hall of Australia, Pty. Ltd., Sydney
Prentice-Hall of Canada, Ltd., Toronto
Prentice-Hall of India Private Ltd., New Delhi
Prentice-Hall of Japan, Inc., Tokyo

10 9 8 7 6 5 4 3 2 1

Library of Congress Cataloging in Publication Data

Aaron, Henry, 1934-
  Hitting the Aaron way.

SUMMARY: The most effective techniques in hitting a
baseball are described by Hank Aaron who is expected to
surpass Babe Ruth's home run record in 1974.
    1. Batting (Baseball)—Juvenile literature.
2. Aaron, Henry, 1934-   —Juvenile literature.
[1. Batting (Baseball)   2. Aaron, Henry, 1934-   ]
I. Cohen, Joel H., joint author. II. Title.
GV869.A27   796.357'26   74-5345
ISBN 0-13-392407-6

CONTENTS

HITTING THE AARON WAY

Hank Leads Off

If you're anything like me, you really love baseball. I've loved the game for as long as I can remember. Every chance I got when I was your age, I was on the ballfield hitting a baseball, or throwing or catching one.

Even today, every aspect of playing baseball gives me pleasure, and I'd like to be remembered as a player who could do it all. When people talk about Henry Aaron in the future, I hope they'll mention that in a given season he could steal 30 bases, hit 40 home runs and bat .340 or .350, instead of constantly dwelling on the fact that he hit 700-something home runs. And I'd like them to remember not only that I could hit, but that I won several Golden Glove awards for fielding and that I was able to run the bases, that I could play hitters correctly and throw runners out, that I hustled—that I did all the things that other ballplayers appreciate.

Still, I know it's inevitable that I'll be remembered as a hitter. Hitting probably gives the most pleasure of all baseball skills, and it's what I've experienced and learned about hitting that I want to share with you in this book.

No, this book isn't going to turn you into a Hank Aaron or a Willie Mays or a Johnny Bench. But it can help you along the path to better hitting, whatever your playing level or your natural ability.

Which brings up an important point. People always refer to me as a "natural" hitter, and it is true that I've been blessed with certain God-given abilities that help me give pitched balls a pretty good ride. It's also true that natural abilities put limits on how far you can develop as a hitter.

But don't think that because you're not a "natural" you can't improve. Everyone—including the "naturals"—can hit better, if he's dedicated, willing to learn and master the fundamentals, willing to take advice and work hard and long, to develop his talents to the maximum.

The fact that you're reading this shows you're interested in learning, so welcome. But a few words of warning:

Obviously a book can only suggest what to do, and it's *doing* what you've read and what your coach or manager tells you that will bring results.

Also, keep in mind that what is good advice for a major-leaguer may be a little too advanced for a younger player in Little League or elsewhere. So read with care and, in any case, be guided by what your coach tells you. After all, he knows you personally and can tell you what's best suited to *you*.

Some of the things I do in baseball are unorthodox and not recommended for most players. So here and there you'll see some advice in the category of "do-what-I-say-not-what-I-do."

Remember that major-leaguers who have done well with hitches in their swings, contortions at the plate, strange stances, lifted front foot, etc., are the exceptions. So if you must imitate somebody's batting style, try to stay with the more normal hitting players.

Some of what I talk about is geared to long-ball hitting. But, as we'll discuss in some detail, that doesn't mean everyone should try to be a slugger. The sluggers get the publicity, but the singles hitters and the others make their important contributions to their teams, too. Knowing what you can or can't do as a hitter, and then capitalizing on your ability, is a long step toward better hitting.

Above all, don't forget that baseball (especially at the level you're playing it now) is a game, something to be enjoyed. A lot of the pleasure of playing comes, of course, from sharpening your skills to the maximum and doing your best to win. But mastery of the fundamentals comes first, so that, win or lose, you know you've given your best.

I hope this book can help you achieve that. . . .

Sincerely,

Hank Aaron

Showdown

It's the bottom of the ninth and your team is trailing by a run. With two outs a teammate socks a double down the left-field line, and now it's all up to you. A hit will tie the game, a home run will win it. And nobody has to remind you that you make an out and it's all over.

So you've got a tough mission. Your heart is pounding, but you step to the plate with confidence. You shut out the crowd noise, while your mind, like a super computer, in a split second sizes up the game situation, the kind of pitcher you're facing, what he's been throwing to you. You set yourself for the pitch. Now the battle has narrowed down to two people: you the batter, and the "enemy" on the mound, the pitcher who'll use all his skill and cunning to get you out.

Maybe you haven't faced situations quite so dramatic, but they do crop up—in World Series games, in Little League contests, in choose-up-sides games on your neighborhood sandlot. And always, the factors are essentially the same. Whether or not you get the crucial hit depends on everything you've learned—from fundamentals to strategy—and everything you've done—from endless practice sessions to actual game situations—before you step to the plate.

Let's discuss those elements that will help you get the hit.

1
The Bat

BAT IS TO BATTER AS . . .

His bat is to a batter as an ax is to a woodsman or a scalpel to a surgeon. The skill of the man wielding the instrument is the key factor, but he wants his instrument to be as ideal for him as possible. The same holds true in your selection of a bat. Make sure it's right—for you.

HEAVY DOESN'T ALWAYS MEAN FAR

Put a half-dozen bats that vary in weight from, say, 30 to 40 ounces, and ask a group of your friends to pick out the one they think will enable them to drive a baseball the greatest distance. I'll bet almost everyone picks the heaviest, thinking he can do more damage to a ball with that bat.

So many young players think they can hit a ball harder and farther with a heavy bat, say, 40 ounces, than one that is 10 ounces lighter. This simply isn't true. I use a 33- or 34-ounce bat (35 inches long) that feels very comfortable in my hands, and I believe I get the same distance out of it that I could with a heavy one. All I want the ball to do is go over the fence, or at least be hit hard and safely someplace, and my bat does the job.

There's a negative side to using a bat that's too heavy.

As you know, in a sport like baseball or golf or tennis, it's vital to "keep your eye on the ball"—that is, watch it without interruption as you prepare to hit it. Using too heavy a bat makes you jerk your head so that you take your eye off the ball, a fatal hitting error. It also makes you move your hands improperly, with the result that you're defeating what you should be doing at the plate.

So what weight bat do I suggest you use? One that feels comfortable to you.

I don't think that up to age seventeen you can comfortably handle a bat that weighs more than 30 ounces. With anything heavier, you're likely to run into trouble. Also, most pitches you'll see will be fastballs, another good reason for using a light bat.

I generally swing a 33-ouncer, which sometimes feels like Ralph Garr's bat in my hands. Some days your 30-ounce bat is going to feel like 40 ounces; other days it will feel light; and most times—if you get used to it—just right. So pick up a bat that weighs 30 ounces or a little less and, if it feels comfortable, stick with it. Remember, by being quicker with a light bat you get the same result as with a heavy bat.

As I mentioned above, I usually use a 33-ounce bat but sometimes move to a 34-ouncer. When I was much younger, I used to change bats, depending on who was pitching. If, for example, it was someone who was throwing a lot of junk, I'd take a heavier bat and try to slow my hands down. In a slump, I've picked up a heavier bat to slow my hands down and keep my head from moving; then, when I'm back in the hitting groove, I pick up the regular bat again. This all comes from experience.

In your competition, though, the pitcher is likely to be just trying to throw the ball and trying to work on his stuff. So I don't advise you to change bats for a particular circumstance.

In the minors I used a bigger-barreled bat than I do now. For about the last seventeen years I've been using the same bat model (63-A), varying just an ounce in weight. I'll use the lighter one when I'm a little tired, such as when we've played sixteen or seventeen games and traveled a lot. You'd be surprised what a difference that ounce makes.

OTHER BAT FACTORS

Weight isn't the only factor to consider in picking a bat. Some bats are shaped differently; two bats can weigh the same but have their weight distributed differently. Both shape and weight distribution will affect how comfortable you are with a particular bat.

Shape

The bat I use has the weight distributed equally, all the way down from the barrel almost to the knob. It's a very, very thin bat, built like an S-2. My bat is not quite as big as the D-89, Joe DiMaggio's model, al-

15

though the handle is a little bigger. The reason I use a bat like that is the fact that I have very large hands, and if I use a thin-handled bat, I'll be forced to grip the bat too tight, and the first thing I know I'll start digging my nails into my skin.

If you happen to have big hands, try a D-89 model, 30 ounces; or my model, 63-A, which weighs 30 ounces, or an S-2 of the same weight. The bat style I use may not feel good to you. Select one that does.

GRIPPING A BAT

There are several ways to hold a bat, and again your comfort is a good indicator of what's best.

Where on You

I like to hold the bat well back in the palm of my hand, down in the large (fleshy) part of the thumb, with the knob of the bat lying right beneath the palm of my hand. Another way, one that's popular with many high-school coaches, is to hold it in your fingers.

Even as a young stringbean of a player I was blessed with very strong wrists, which helped me to be a natural wrist hitter.

16

Now, the reason I hold the bat well back in my hand, instead of in my fingers, is that basically I'm a wrist hitter. Holding it back there gives me a grip that allows me to roll my wrists and, in a sense, "throw" the bat at the ball. Gripping the bat in my fingers would make that roll kind of tough to do, since I'd be locking my wrists.

Don't worry if you're not a wrist hitter. That's something that comes naturally. It's a gift from God. And if you aren't blessed with that gift, you can still work on being strong with your wrists (see section on PRACTICE), even though you probably won't be able to do everything with them that some natural hitters can.

(Incidentally, part of my good wrist development came about as a result of the cross-handed grip with which I held the bat for many years. In the cross-handed grip, which is absolutely wrong, I stood as right-handed hitters do, with my left side toward the pitcher, but my left hand was *above* my right on the bat. It was a long time before anyone corrected me—and, I have to confess, there were times after I was corrected that I'd sneak my left hand back on top when I got in a jam because I felt more secure. But although I'd done well and hit with power with that unorthodox grip, and although it helped develop my wrists, a cross-handed grip is a no-no. It's a dangerous way to hit—an inside pitch can crack your wrist. And it's going to cost you a lot of points on your batting average.)

Where on the Bat

I like to hold the bat down near the knob for maximum power. This is called the *full-length* or *end* grip. Others hold the bat an inch and a half or two inches from the end, for a combination of power and bat-control. This is called either the *modified full-length* or the *modified choke grip*. And some *choke up*, that is, they keep their hands quite a bit up on the handle, for maximum bat-control.

Hold the bat at the point where it lets you feel the quickest. It's likely that at your age choking up will enable you to handle a bat most effectively. You'll be able to punch the ball or hit it to your power field, because you'll be able to control the bat better.

Ted Williams, who seldom used a bat heavier than 34 ounces, once picked up a 34½-ounce weapon. Instead of holding it down at the end, he choked up some and began getting hits to left field in spaces his opponents left by putting on extreme fielding shifts against him. Ted wasn't getting around as fast with the heavier bat, but choking up on it worked very well

17

FIG. 1 A modified full-length grip, about two inches from the end of the bat, gives you a combination of power and bat control.

Fig. 1

FIG. 2 For maximum bat control, *choke up* on the bat—hold it quite a distance up from the handle.

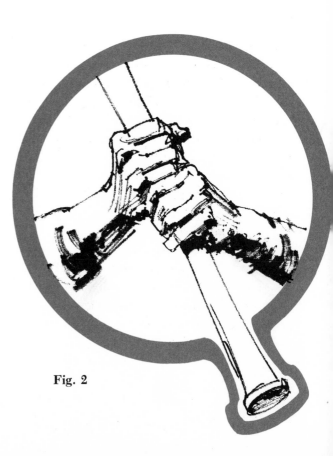

Fig. 2

against the shift. After a while, opposing fielders began spreading out more against Ted, so he switched back to a lighter bat, resumed his normal grip and began pulling the ball again. Later in his career he never went to the opposite field.

One man I played with, Red Schoendienst, got results with his choked-grip swing that were as good as I got with mine. He could hit a long ball that way because he stood right on top of the plate. If he did not stand that close, I'm sure he would have held the bat down at the end.

Most hitters who choke up, though, don't hit the long ball. They choke up on the bat because it gives them better bat-control. They hit for average rather than distance, and still are great assets to their teams. An excellent example is Felix Millan, who used to be my teammate on the Braves before going to the Mets. He chokes way up on the bat, and he's a master at stroking the ball for base hits—183 of them in 1970, and 185 in 1973 for a .290 average.

Where *you* should hold the bat is something you've got to figure out yourself by working on it. You've got to experiment holding it different ways, and then stick with what gives you the most consistency and power.

TOUCHING HANDS

Most hitters have their hands touching when they hold a bat, but not all. My hands touch each other, the outer edge of the right hand in contact with the inner edge of the left below. But I've seen some players who leave space between their hands, and they're pretty fair hitters. Billy Williams is one of them. Meanwhile, Willie Stargell interlocks a couple of fingers—the pinky of his left hand (top hand for a left-handed hitter, which Willie is), and the index finger of his right.

So once again, there's no single right way to do it. It all goes back to how you adjust best at the plate. Finding out whether your hands should touch, whether they should be kept a little apart or whether your fingers should interlock takes practice. Whichever way you hold the bat, it's advisable that the middle knuckles of your top hand never be lined up forward of the base knuckles of the bottom hand.

TIGHT, LOOSE

19

How tightly do you hold the bat?
One of the greatest hitters I had the pleasure of playing against was

Stan Musial. He said you'll find that the hands of most good hitters are so loose when they get to the plate, anybody could come up and pick the bat right out of their hands.

I like to keep my left hand loose on the bat just before the pitch, and then tighten it up just a bit, because the right hand loosens up as the pitch comes in.

For a right-handed hitter, the right hand is actually the guide, while the left provides the power. So if you're a right-handed batter, pick up the bat with your left hand and make sure it feels comfortable to you. (By the way, I've seen hitters with physical power pick up a bat with one hand and hit the ball out of the park.) When I go to the plate, I pick the bat up with my left hand and make sure the label is pointed directly at my face.

Speaking of labels, there is a story told about me, which isn't true, that one time in the 1957 World Series I came up to bat against the Yankees and Yogi Berra, who's now manager of the Mets, was catching. To rattle me, the story goes, he said, "Hey, kid, you're holding the bat wrong; it's supposed to be with the label up." And I supposedly answered, "I didn't come here to read," and then got a base hit.

That story aside, you should hold the bat with the label up, not because the bat will split if you don't, but to make sure that there's good wood at the point where the bat and ball meet. So keep the label in your face as you wait and make sure you hit the ball with the label pointed toward the catcher.

As you can tell, there are many different ways you can hold a bat, many ways you can control it. Obviously, the most important thing is the result.

BATTING GLOVES

Batting gloves have become popular in the last couple of years. I don't know whether some players wear them to take the sting out of their hands or just for the sake of wearing them.

At the beginning of the season I like to wear a glove because the bat causes a blister on my left hand. I'll wear a glove once or twice a game, depending on how sore the blister gets. But once it gets well, I don't like to wear a batting glove, for the simple reason that I like to feel the bat in my hands.

2
Stance, Stride, Strike Zone

STANCE

It's important to have your entire body in the right position when you get up at bat. Right position for *you*, of course, is most important, but there are certain principles that apply to everybody.

One thing you have to have is control of your upper body. Make sure your front shoulder (the left if you're a right-handed hitter) is aimed directly at the pitcher. When you get into the batter's box, you should always square yourself up with the pitcher. Your front shoulder shouldn't dip; even if you've got a bend in your knees, you've still got to keep your shoulders square.

Also, it's important to keep your elbows and arms away from your body. Only an awfully quick swinger can hit successfully with his arms locked into him. But if your elbows are away so that you can swing freely, you'll be able to pull the ball to left field or push it to right or sock it through the middle, provided, of course, you concentrate on the pitch.

This, too, is something you'll have to learn through your own experience. There will always be an exception someone will cite who held his bat very close to his body and did well as a hitter. But you're not going to find too many good hitters who held the bat close, so hold it away and concentrate.

BATTER'S BOX

A major-league batter's box is six feet long and four feet wide. Many hitters like to stand in front of the plate because they want to hit the curve ball before it breaks. I prefer to stand a little behind the plate because I want to see the curve ball *when* it breaks, and then decide whether to swing and where to swing.

If you decide on standing well back in the box, it means you'll have to learn to go into the ball. The reason for this will be apparent in professional ball, where pitchers have such great control that if you stand way back and don't step into it, pitchers will just tear you apart with pitches on the outside corner.

Bat Coverage

Whether you're in the back of the batter's box, in front of it or even with the plate, once you commit yourself and take your stride, you have to make sure that the meat part of your bat is completely covering all parts of the plate.

Foot Position

Where you stand in the box is one part of batting stance. How you position your feet is another. No matter what part of the box you're standing in, there are three basic stances: the *parallel* or *square* stance, the *open* and the *closed*.

In the *parallel* or *square* stance, your feet are about equally distant from the plate, parallel to each other and at right angles to the sides of the batter's box. Many players using this stance turn their front foot toward the pitcher just a bit.

In the *open* stance, your front foot—the one nearer the pitcher—is farther away from the plate than your back foot.

In the *closed* stance, your back foot is farther away from the plate than your front foot.

The open stance favors pull hitting; the closed is usually better for hitting straightaway.

Sometimes if you find you're having trouble hitting an outside pitch, you might want to open your stance a bit and move closer to the plate.

I prefer a medium open stance, not too close to the plate, but close enough so I'll be able to stride and hit a pitch over the outside part of the plate while still protecting the inside.

FIG. 3 Stand close enough to the plate so that the "meat" part of the bat can hit a pitch over any portion of the plate, even the outside corner.

24

FIG. 4 When you stand too far from the plate, the thick business part of your bat is too far inside.

FIG. 5 The closed stance, in which your front foot is nearer the plate than your back foot, is good for hitting the ball straightaway.

FIG. 6 The open stance, in which your front foot is farther away from the plate than your back foot, is good for pulling the ball to your power field.

Stepping Out of the Box

When the pitcher takes a long time to throw, probably in an attempt to get you nervous, it's wise to step out of the box and let him wait. (Make sure you ask the umpire to call time first.) But beware about stepping out of the box when you swing. Years ago when Bob Uecker was catching for the Cardinals, he kept telling the umpire I was stepping out of the front part of the batter's box as I swung. Then on one at-bat, Curt Simmons threw me a change-up and I eagerly took a step toward the mound and hit the ball out of the park. But my home run never counted because the umpire called me out for being out of the box.

DIGGING IN

Some players rub their rear foot back and forth in the ground in the batter's box. Possibly this "digging-in" at the plate gives them confidence and shows the pitcher they're not going to be intimidated. But you'll never see me digging in, because I feel that I'd be locking myself in by doing it. So I always like to keep my foot on the ground.

KNEE BENDS

Sometimes I like to stand at the plate with a little bend in my knees. That's mostly just to concentrate on not swinging at the low pitch, and not overswinging at the high pitch. It's to make the pitcher get it in the strike zone.

As a rule, you should bend your knees slightly, keep your hips, eyes and shoulders level and have your weight evenly distributed on the balls of your feet. I keep my feet a normal distance apart so I won't overstride or understride. I want to make sure that when I stride, I'm going to have enough power left in my bat to hit the ball hard.

COPYING

As with other fundamentals of baseball, it's a mistake to copy somebody's stance just because it looks good and he gets good results with it. It may not work for you. What you can do is *try* another player's stance.

27

For that matter, try *everybody's* stance. Once you get one that feels comfortable, that's the stance you should use.

Don't seek out an unorthodox stance. On the other hand, don't be put off by one that's awkward-looking. You see major-leaguers with all types of stances—legs wide apart; deep crouches; strange ways of holding the bat; some so bent over it looks impossible to throw a strike to them—and yet many of them do well. Stan Musial had a distinguished career standing way back in the batter's box coiled in a deep crouch. A lot of professional players and other so-called experts predicted he'd never be able to hit that way, yet "The Man" had well over 3,000 hits in his career.

WHY ARE YOU STANDING AWAY FROM THE PLATE?

If you're standing far away from the plate, you might ask yourself why. Be honest. Is it because you're afraid of being hit? If so, you're not alone. A lot of youngsters don't want to stand up near the plate. And let's face it. The prospect of a strong young athlete standing on a mound just 60½ feet away from you and throwing a hardball in your direction isn't likely to relax you.

Even major-league players experience butterflies. (Paul Blair of the Orioles was hit by a pitched ball, and after he recovered he underwent hypnosis to get over his new tendency to duck away from pitches.) Really, though, you shouldn't ever think of being hit when you're at the plate. Instead, you should go up there thinking you're going to get a ball over the middle of the plate and hit it.

I've been hit several times by pitches—twice in the head and several times in the back. Frank Robinson, I think, for years, led the league in being struck, but he really didn't care about that. He was determined to stand where he wanted to stand, and was a very successful hitter doing it.

Of course, it's awfully tough for me to tell you not to worry about being hit. But, speaking as one who knows what it's like, and having seen other players struck, I can assure you it only hurts for a little while. I don't think you can get seriously hurt.

As a kid, I was lucky because fear never influenced my playing. This may be hard to believe, but I can remember going in back of the plate and catching a hardball wearing only a mask and glove—no cup, no chest protector or any other protective gear. That doesn't mean I wouldn't have worn a batting helmet at the plate if helmets were in existence when I was

FIG. 7 Fear of the ball can lead to putting your "foot in the bucket"—awkwardly stepping back from the plate with your back foot and twisting your body. Go to the plate confident that you're going to hit the ball, not the other way around.

a kid. Don't go to the plate unless you've got your headgear on, because accidents can happen. In the major leagues, I always wear my helmet. The reason I don't put it on until the last minute when I step into the box is that it's heavy. And I want to make sure the pitcher sees me putting it on.

It's difficult to tell whether a pitcher ever hits a batter deliberately—there's such a fine line between a beanball and a pitch to brush the hitter back. Sometimes a pitcher could just be throwing up and in on a hitter who is leaning over the plate guessing for something else.

In my early years I was thrown at, and once I made the mistake of saying I would retaliate by throwing a bat or something like that. But it was wrong to show their tactics bothered me. The best way to get even is to just get up there and knock the daylights out of the next pitch. That will eliminate the knockdown pitch, because it shows it doesn't bother you. I generally respect a pitcher for throwing a close pitch, providing he can control it. Don Drysdale used to throw inside on me a lot to get me away from the plate, but he never hit me, even though he could have if he'd wanted to. If the ball does hit you, you've got to just shake it off and keep going.

A really good pitcher who gets an 0-2 count on a batter knows he shouldn't throw a strike on the next pitch, but it should be close enough to give the batter something to think about. He'll either brush the hitter back with an inside fastball or throw one outside, and, either way, he's not going to miss by much. The good pitchers have a purpose when they throw—and they can control it.

In your league, the pitchers aren't as much in control of what they throw as the hurlers are in the majors (and even some of *them* are affectionately known as wildmen), so be alert. But don't let fear get into the batter's box with you. One suggestion I've read is to start out with an unorthodox stance in which you're just about facing the pitcher in order to gain confidence. But that isn't going to establish good hitting patterns. Ted Williams, one of the greatest hitters I ever saw, said that in order to be a good hitter you have to concentrate on the ball and forget about the fear. Certainly, you can't expect to be a successful professional ballplayer if every time you come to the plate you're saying to yourself, "Uh-oh, he may hit me." You've got to conquer that fear. I'd say that one way to keep your head in the batter's box without worrying about being hit by the pitch is just to try to hit the ball right back through the middle. That way, I think, you will concentrate.

If I told you *not* to think of elephants, you'd have a hard time thinking of anything *but* elephants. And so you may see no more value than that in my saying you've got to get over your fear by not worrying about it. But really, that's what I am suggesting.

Just as I tell youngsters running the bases to slide without hesitation to avoid breaking a leg, I'm telling those of you who are afraid, to unhesitatingly go up to the plate determined to hit the ball. As I said before, if you concentrate on seeing and hitting the ball you won't have a chance to remember you're afraid. And even if it should be thrown at you, nine times out of ten you'll get out of the way in time.

So don't let fear keep you away from the plate. Keep relaxed and act confident in the batter's box. (Don't be overconfident, though, or so determined to prove you're not afraid that you take unnecessary risks like leaning your head over the plate.)

GETTING SET TO HIT

Okay, you're standing in the batter's box poised for the pitch. Your weight is evenly distributed on the balls of your feet; you don't want to be back on your heels. Your stance is comfortable. You're close enough to the plate so that the fat part of the bat can make contact with the ball over the outside corner, and your stance is such that you can also handle an inside pitch.

How high should you hold your bat? Jackie Robinson used to hold it way up and back. Bobby Tolan likes to hold it way up above his head. Mel Ott's hands were way down low, almost at the belt. Ted Williams liked his hands just a little below shoulder level. He suggested that if a hitter wanted to be a little quicker getting on top of the ball pitched high, he could raise his hands. Most hitters hold the bat with their hands about shoulder-high (at the rear shoulder, of course) because they feel it gives them good control for high or low pitches. Most batters hold their forward arm roughly parallel to the ground, and the elbow of the rear arm slightly below the shoulder.

As you await the start of the pitcher's delivery, you probably move your bat once or twice through the arc where you'd like to hit. But then as the pitcher prepares to throw, your bat should be still. I have a hitch in my batting swing. When I'm getting ready to hit, I kind of wiggle my bat around. I'm able to recover, but it's wrong to be moving your bat, so I give the advice that I received when I was young: Just hold your bat still. Don't let your hands dip as the ball is pitched, because if you don't bring them back up in time, your swing will be flawed by a hitch. Also, don't let the hitting part of your bat hang below your shoulders.

You don't swing a bat pushing forward from a dead stop. To swing forward fluidly—to get some muscle in your swing—you've got to have some kind of backward motion. But—and this is important—you should never have a back*swing*, because then you've got too far to recover.

In other words, keep that backward movement to a minimum. The least amount of hitch or backswing you have in your bat, the better the connection you're going to make with the ball. But if you start off with a decided hitch, the first thing you're going to be doing is start dropping your hands and backswinging, and you're just not going to be able to recuperate in time. So always concentrate on starting that bat forward.

You'll see some batters resting the bat on their shoulders as they wait. I don't recommend it, because every split second counts. Have it ready to swing in a level, flat arc.

Ted Williams thought the hands should be relatively close to the body. As I mentioned earlier, I think they should be well away.

You'll see hitters who stand straight; some who bend a little; others who bend a lot and have their rears way out.

I like to crouch just a little bit with a slight bend in my knees.

EYE ON THE BALL

Possibly the most important of all hitting fundamentals is keeping your eye on the ball. Obviously, you're not going to hit the ball if you're looking somewhere else. You've got to be right with the pitch. In fact, you should be watching the pitcher's arm as it comes around, getting your sights on the ball from that point on, to try to pick up its speed and spin and to determine whether it's a fastball or breaking pitch.

Sometimes I can actually see the bat hit the ball. That happens if I go along for a month really hitting the ball squarely.

Your head should be still. Be careful not to jerk it as some players do. Although some batters may drop the front shoulder a little to handle a low pitch, your shoulders should be kept as even as possible. At least they should start out level.

I make sure the length of my stride enables me to be well-balanced throughout my swing—in this case it helped produce my 700th home run.

STRIDE

As the ball is pitched, you take a stride toward the pitcher with your front foot. Whether you realize it or not, though, your stride involves more than just that foot or leg. In a way, your whole body is part of the striding motion. As you step forward, make sure you go into the ball. But to help your timing and to hit a ball where it's pitched, don't plant that foot until you've decided where and what the pitch is.

With your stride, your weight will shift somewhat to the back foot. However, I don't think you should put much more weight on your back leg, because if you do you're going to have a tendency to bring your front shoulder up and possibly lose sight of the ball.

Except for a slight movement needed to help you keep balance, your head stays still. But your hips begin pivoting backward, along with your shoulders, arms and hands. Turning your front knee in a bit helps the backward rotation of your hips.

It's important at this point that you've got the bat back, because, although you've made your stride, you still haven't decided whether or not to swing at the pitch. If you decide to swing, and you've already made your

33

Too long a stride causes your shoulder to dip with a resulting loss in smoothness and power.

stride and brought your bat forward, you're not going to be able to deal effectively with a change-up. Holding your bat back as you stride lets you wait on the ball.

Be careful not to *over*stride.

With a relatively short stride, you can attack the ball better, because you can pick up the movement of the ball and watch it better. And this contributes to better bat-control.

There's another point to consider, too: If you're striding correctly, the distribution of your weight will be even and so will the line of your shoulders. Otherwise, you might tend to be way back on your back foot and your bat will be dropping and your shoulder will be way up in the air. As a result, you're just not going to be picking the ball up as well as if you had taken a short or medium stride.

How to overcome the tendency to overstride?

One thing we do in spring training is have a batter draw a line in the batter's box with a bat to see where his stride takes him in relation to his starting position. You might do that.

Another common suggestion is to spread your legs a little wider when you come up to bat. This not only prevents a long stride, but also cuts

Fig. 8

FIG. 8-10 Overstriding, a common fault of young hitters, causes your shoulders to move into the ball before your hips do. The result frequently is that your shoulders are uneven, you're off-balance, and you lack the power for solid contact with the ball.

36

Fig. 9

Fig. 10

38   Fig. 11

FIG. 11-13 When the stride is too short, your hips turn into the ball before the shoulders, and your swing is cramped instead of being fluid as it should be.

Fig. 12

40　　Fig. 13

down the likelihood of an early step and pulling your body away from the plate. It will also limit your ability to step into a pitch, though.

Making your step early will usually lead to pulling a ball, hitting it to your power field (left field if you're a right-handed hitter, right field for a lefty). This isn't necessarily bad if you're a fastball hitter and the pitch is a fastball. But because an early stride transfers some of your weight from the back foot too soon, it weakens your ability to hit a curve or slow pitch.

COILED SPRING

The reason you pivot your hips, shoulders, arms and hands backward as you prepare to swing is based on the same principle as that of a coiled spring. Wind it up correctly and it can be released with lightning power.

The pitch is on its way. You've made your stride and coiled your power rearward. It looks as if the pitch is in your strike zone and you've decided to swing at it. You uncoil your power. Your hips begin opening toward the pitcher, as you push off your rear foot; your shoulders open and your arms and hands spring forward, drawn by your hips. Your bat, flattening out in a level arc toward the pitch, follows your hands, with the speed increasing as you get closer to the hitting area. Your weight shifts to your front foot, and you whip the bat into the ball.

How much power you bring to the swing will depend in great measure on how well and quickly your hips and arms rotate. Maximum power depends on their quick action, so they've got to swing free. On inside pitches, it's advisable to bring them around particularly quickly.

The quicker you are with the bat, the longer you can wait on a pitch and the less likely you are to be fooled. Bat speed is especially important when you're swinging at a slowball. Some people recommend swinging at the last possible instant. I've done it a lot of times. Ted Williams was a master at it.

Batting in Little League or other amateur baseball competition is a different matter. There the pitchers come and go, whereas in the big leagues I've been looking at some of the same pitchers for a dozen or more years and I have a basic idea of what they're throwing. I'm sure Ted Williams knew as much about the pitchers he was facing as they knew about him.

41

42 Fig. 14

FIG. 14-17 When you're striding properly, your weight will be evenly distributed, your shoulders will be in line, and your whole body will uncoil smoothly and powerfully as you lean into the pitch and connect for a hit. Good stride usually results in a clean, arms-extended follow-through.

Fig. 15

43

44   Fig. 16

Fig. 17

45

This swing produced my 600th home run, but most importantly, notice the level position of my arms and bat—this illustrates when I mean about swinging down on the ball.

So what I recommend is that you learn to get the bat around as quickly as you can. This doesn't mean that you necessarily commit yourself too early on the pitch. Just get ready to swing your bat at something hard like a fastball or slider or curve.

The ability to hold back until the last moment will come to you over a period of years—but, say, until you're seventeen, you should just concentrate on being quick with the bat.

SWING DOWN

Different players have different attitudes about swinging—up, down or level with the ground. Some suggest swinging down on high pitches, up at low. Others almost always take an uppercut, and some of them aren't even long-ball hitters. Ted Williams advocated a slight upswing. I think you should learn to swing down.

This may sound funny, but what that kind of a swing does is give you rotation on the ball, a backward rotation or backspin, so that even when it's hit in the infield, it picks up speed and scoots on through—on natural

46

WIDE WORLD PHOTOS

Here I am swinging up at the ball (something I suggest you avoid) against Tom Seaver. It worked out all right here—a home run—but this doesn't happen that often against Tom.

I swung down on the ball when I hit this home run (#703) against the Montreal Expos. Swinging down helps me hit the ball solidly and consistently.

47

WIDE WORLD PHOTOS

ground. And when you hit the ball in the air with a down swing, it has that backspin and carries a little farther. Hitting down, or "tomahawking," as some refer to it, may cost you some distance, but it will pay off in hard ground balls and line drives to the outfield. When I'm swinging the bat well, that's the way I swing—down on the ball.

HIT BALL OUT FRONT

I try to hit the ball out in front of the plate, and so should you. This, of course, takes quickness with the bat. If you can acquire the quickness you'll be able to handle the ball whether it's inside or out and hit with maximum power.

Some experts suggest that you aim through the pitcher's box, so if the pitch is inside, a quick stride and swing can be made to pull the ball; and if the pitch is outside, you can swing later and drive the ball to the opposite field.

FOLLOW THROUGH

For the best results, you can't halt your swing at the point of impact. When you hit the ball, follow through with everything you've got. As soon as the bat impacts with the ball, your wrists should break or snap in line with your swing and your arms should continue through that arc until they're fully extended. If you choke up, you'll be moving your arms a shorter distance than someone with an end grip.

If you've swung correctly, you'll end your follow-through leaning in the direction of where you've hit the ball, perfectly balanced. The front foot will be planted solidly, while only the toes of your back foot are likely to be in contact with the ground. Your rear knee will be bent quite a bit.

You've got to keep your head down as you swing and follow through. Jerking it away will upset the smoothness of your swing.

It's taken several pages to talk about it, but the entire swing, from stride to follow-through is a matter of a second or two. In fact, you've got just a fraction of a second to make up your mind whether or not to swing. You need concentration and quickness.

48

BE AGGRESSIVE

Another quality you need is aggressiveness. I'm not talking about walking around with a chip on your shoulder looking for a fight. I'm talking about being an aggressive batter at the plate.

To be a good hitter, you can't be lazy with your body or brain. You've got to be ready to attack the ball. You can't wait for it to be right on top of you; you've got to go out and get it.

Being aggressive means that when you get to the plate and the pitcher is winding up, you make sure you're going after the ball instead of letting the ball come after you. You hit it in front, rather than behind.

Aggressiveness means knowing what you want to do when you get to the plate, what pitch you want to hit. Most good hitters—Stan Musial, Jackie Robinson, Frank Robinson, Ted Williams, Willie Mays—were aggressive at the plate. Watching them, you had to know that a good hitter can't be lazy. You can't stand waiting for a pitch to be exactly down the middle. In the big leagues, certainly, you're not going to get that kind of pitch. So train yourself to stride properly and don't thrust your bat forward too soon.

It helps to be looking for—expecting—the fastball all the time. But be able to hit the curve or change-up if it should show up instead.

I think I'm more of an aggressive hitter when there are men on base. I bear down a little more, and maybe as a result the pitcher is the one who feels the pressure.

So be aggressive at the plate, and remember that no matter how big or small you are, it will help you become a good hitter.

KNOW YOUR STRIKE ZONE

In a game against the New York Mets during the 1973 season I hit two home runs on pitches that were thrown out of the strike zone. In the 1957 World Series, Don Larsen of the Yankees threw me a fastball high and outside the strike zone and I drove it over the barrier in right-center.

In twenty seasons of major-league baseball, I've hit quite a few "bad" balls for home runs. But this is another one of those subjects in which I strongly advise you *not* to follow my example. (Sure, hit home runs if you can, but don't swing at bad balls.)

49

It's important to keep your eye on the ball from the instant it leaves the pitcher's hand. Make sure you keep your arms enough away from your body that you can swing freely and comfortably.

Notice the way I keep my head down on the ball, moving it as little as possible."

As my front foot starts to move, I cock my hips back.

Then my hips and bat uncoil as I stride toward the ball.

Notice my complete follow-through which assures smoothness in my swing.

Hitting the homer was fun for me, but I don't think the catcher enjoyed it much.

A

B

C

D

E

F

G

H

I

J

K

Instead, I strongly recommend that you learn your strike zone and wait for the pitch—in the zone—that you can hit best. The earlier you learn the strike zone, and the earlier you learn patience at the plate, the better off you'll be. (The strike zone is roughly the area over the plate between your armpits and the top of your knees when you take your normal stance. Because of different positions umpires take up in the National and American leagues to call balls and strikes, National League umps call a "low" strike and American Leaguers a "high" strike.)

Remember, a pitcher has to throw three strikes to get you out, and I feel no matter who is on the mound, he's going to have to give you one pitch to hit within the strike zone. It may not be your favorite pitch, but it will be one to hit.

You don't want to be overanxious at bat, but too much patience can also be a handicap. Here's what I mean: There are times when pitches are in the strike zone and the hitter doesn't want to swing, preferring to wait for "his" pitch, the type and location and speed he handles best.

I've often done that—played the waiting game—on the theory that it takes just one to get a hit. And so, even with the count 3-2, I consider myself ahead of the pitcher. Often it's worth it to wait for the ball that's in my "happy zone," as Ted Williams called it, a ball in the area where I can hit most solidly and effectively.

But even though I've held back on strikes, with good success, I don't recommend it to you. If you're looking for a curve ball and it's in the strike zone, swing at it. You may not get a better one to hit this time at bat. Keep in mind that when I'm at the plate I'm looking at pitchers I've seen and studied over a period of years. I know that every time I get up I'm going to get at least one pitch I can hit.

When there's a pitcher on the mound I've never seen, I may lay off several strikes while studying him. Especially the first time up, I'll definitely watch him closely to see what kind of fastball he's throwing, what kind of breaking pitch, and so forth. I like to know what his best pitch is, whether he likes to throw the slider or curve ball or change-up for a strike. Then, if I can be patient enough to wait and know whether he's got good control on one type of pitch, I think I can get a pitch that I can hit out of the ballpark.

You should know your own strike zone, and know what pitch you want to hit at all times, be patient enough to wait on your pitch, then make sure you hit hard.

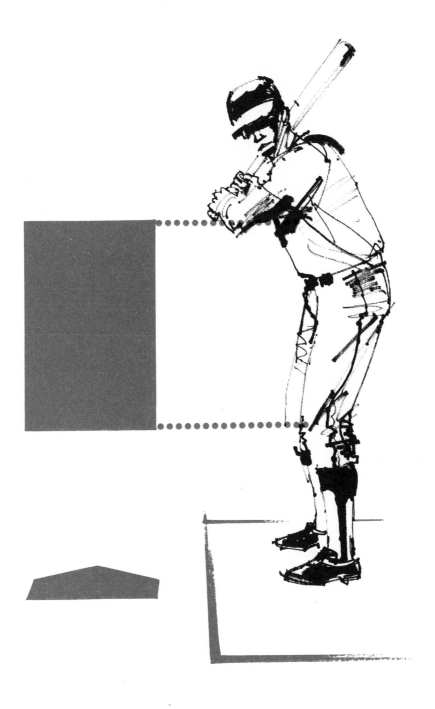

53

FIG. 18 Knowing your strike zone, the area over the plate that's roughly from your knees to your armpits, is fundamental to good hitting.

Learning About Pitchers Yourself

There are things you can learn about a pitcher even before you step to the plate, if you concentrate and don't allow yourself to be distracted.

When your team is up, watch the opposing pitcher throw—not so much to see how he's pitching to your teammates, but to discover what "philosophy" he has on his fastball, what kind of curve he has. The fastball that one pitcher throws is not necessarily the same as the one thrown by another. (By the way, you may find you're able to hit the pitcher who throws a harder fastball better than you do someone who throws it a little softer.)

Some players try to study pitchers for some kind of gesture or other tip-off they may give unconsciously that can alert the hitter to the kind of pitch that's coming. But most pitchers are smart, and nowadays young hurlers are being taught more and more how to keep from tipping off anything.

Helping the Umpire

There's an extra advantage for the batter who concentrates on the strike zone. If you make it to the big leagues and you've got a reputation for never swinging at bad balls, even a pitch that's an inch outside, the umpires will start giving you the benefit of the doubt. Ted Williams was a master at this—he probably had the best eye, of any hitter who ever played the game. (Gary Gentry used to complain that close ones to me were called balls because the umpires knew I knew the strike zone and if I let one go by it was probably a ball.)

On the other hand, if you are overanxious at the plate and start swinging at bad balls, pitchers are going to refuse to throw you strikes. And the first thing you know, the umpires are going to start giving the benefit of the doubt to the pitchers and call strikes on any pitches that you take.

So, certainly, there have been good hitters who were notorious for hitting bad balls. Joe "Ducky" Medwick of the old St. Louis Cardinals supposedly even used to swing at balls over his head. They tell one story about him, that he was threatened with a $100 fine if he swung at any more bad pitches. On a 3-2 count, with two outs and the bases loaded, he hit a ninth-innning home run on a ball pitched over his head; his manager supposedly said, "Congratulations. That will cost you a hundred."

54

With your luck, you'd swing at the bad pitch and miss it and have nothing to remember but the fine. So, for now at least, stick with pitches in your zone.

3
Singles or Homers?

Patterning Yourself

You've probably heard other kids say something like, "Gee, I'd like to hit like Hank Aaron or like Willie Mays," or Johnny Bench or Willie Stargell. Maybe you've said it yourself. I certainly don't think there's anything wrong with that kind of ambition—wanting to hit like a particular big-leaguer—but there are dangers in this that you should be aware of. You may want to hit like me—and I appreciate the compliment—but my style might not fit your style, and you'll have to establish your own pattern.

The late Jackie Robinson was my idol. I admired him and wanted to pattern myself after him. But I knew I couldn't hit like Jackie and I couldn't hold my bat like him and be successful, so I had to adopt my own style. I felt he was the most complete ballplayer I'd ever seen. He could rile up opponents in more ways than one. I knew I didn't have that instinct, that ability to get the opposing players riled up and to motivate my own ballclub, but I felt I could do other things.

Others I admired were Stan Musial, Joe DiMaggio and Ted Williams, but I knew that their hitting styles could not be mine. So do your own thing. Find out what kind of a hitter you are and make the most of it.

HOME RUNS NOT FOR EVERYONE

All types of hits and other skills contribute to winning ballgames, but let's face it: home runs are the spectacular part of baseball. They're what get the fans leaping to their feet. The team with the home-run punch is a constant explosive threat. The players who hit them draw the big salaries, and it's their names that become the household words. But—and this may be a tough fact to swallow—you may never be able to hit for distance.

As a young player in 1959 (top) and as a veteran in 1973 (bottom), I managed to get my share of home runs. However, as a younger player I tried more for contact with the ball than for distance. That's my advice to you, too.

56

It doesn't necessarily have anything to do with your size—relatively small men hit a lot of homers and some big players hit very few. If it turns out that you're not cut out for distance hitting, don't let it get you down. There are many ways you can help your team win games without hitting the long ball. You can save a ballgame by playing your position well. At the plate you can concentrate on being a contact hitter—a man who gets on base regularly by way of singles. You can do a lot of helpful things at the plate, such as bunt a man over to scoring position. And once on base you can use your speed and alertness to steal a crucial base. There are many ways you can help to win a game—or even a championship—and those ways are just as important as hitting home runs.

So don't be discouraged if you aren't a long-ball hitter. If you can learn to meet the ball squarely, you'll do your share of getting on base, regardless of your size.

It all comes back to the fundamental principle of doing what you do best. I don't think I ever saw Maury Wills or Richie Ashburn try to hit the ball out of the park. Instead they concentrated on what their abilities and training allowed them to do best. And did they ever contribute!

In 1973, switch-hitting Pete Rose was voted the National League's Most Valuable Player, beating out Willie Stargell, who had hit 44 home runs. Rose, who had hit just five homers during the regular 1973 season, commented: "A lot of guys think you have to be a big home-run hitter to win. This proves you don't."

There were those (Stargell included) who thought that Stargell, with a .299 average and 119 runs batted in to go with his big home-run output, should have won the MVP honor. But everyone had to admire Pete's accomplishments: a .338 batting average to lead the league for the third time, and 230 base hits—tops in the majors. For the last eight seasons Pete hit .300 or better, and in six seasons had more than 200 hits!

He was the first nonpower-hitter to win the MVP award since Maury Wills did it with 104 stolen bases in 1962. Both men are superb examples of how valuable a player, who is not a home-run hitter, can be to his team.

HIT TO ALL FIELDS

Power hitter or not, it's important for you to learn to hit to all fields. Learning that skill will basically give you all the fundamentals of hitting and the right concept about playing the game. If you're able to hit to all fields, you're going to be able to hit for an average.

57

The way the major leagues operate today, you can't hit just one way, to one field, and be able to hit successfully. If, for example, you're a power hitter who consistently pulls to his power field, managers will order shifts on you to close up gaps and you won't be able to hit through the hole as you normally would. If you're able to hit to all fields and they shift on you, then you can—and should—try to hit to the opposite field.

Nowadays, most clubs shift on me, since I've become a pull hitter, and they want to take away what I do best. But at this stage of my career, I don't think it's of benefit to me to try to punch to right. If I start trying to slap the ball to right at my age, I'll lose just a little bit of my quickness with the bat. But if I were younger or in my late teens, I would certainly do it.

As a matter of fact, early in my professional career I was a dead pull hitter, but with a lot of practice I learned to hit to all fields, and that certainly helped me stay in the big leagues.

Speaking of shifts, once in 1969, Dave Bristol, who was then the manager of the Cincinnati Reds, even moved one of his infielders to the outfield, so that there were four outfielders against me. Shifts don't bother me. In fact, they make me concentrate on hitting the ball a little harder. In the course of a season it works to my advantage, because if I hit a ball hard enough, it's going through no matter what kind of shift is on. Once in a while there's an extra advantage to a hitter. For instance, once I took an extra base on a hit up the middle because Pete Rose was toward left-center and I knew he didn't have a chance to throw me out.

But, as I said, you should hit to the opposite field against a shift, and you should practice to be able to hit to *all* fields. The player who can really handle a bat, stroking the ball to left or right as he chooses, is a rare commodity much appreciated by his teammates.

I don't think you can really practice placing hits exactly where you want them, but you can concentrate on hitting to one area. You might want to swing ten times and hit the ball to right, then swing and hit ten to left, another ten up the middle. Practice it enough and when the situation comes up in a game, you'll have a good chance of getting the ball to the general area you're aiming for.

Babe Ruth supposedly pointed to a spot in the stands in the 1932 World Series and, with two strikes on him, hit a home run there. I believe he was pointing, and maybe hoping, but I can't believe he knew he'd hit it there. On a given pitch, I know I can't put the ball exactly where I want to. I can get it to left field, but not center or right since I started pulling the ball.

Fig. 19

FIG. 19-21 If you're a right-handed hitter trying to pull the ball to left field, try to meet the ball out front. Bat quickness helps. When you follow through, your arms should be fully extended and your head and body positioned in the direction of where the ball is headed.

60   Fig. 20

Fig. 21

62   Fig. 22

FIG. 22-24 It's a plus for a young batsman to be able to hit to all fields. A good stride and well-timed swing will get you hits up the middle.

Fig. 23

64 Fig. 24

Opposite-field hitting is particularly valuable for a right-handed hitter. If you want to advance a man from first to third, being able to hit behind the runner to right is an important skill.

One way suggested for opposite-field hitting (for a righty or a lefty) is to shift your feet so that you're facing the desired target area more than you would have with your normal stance. When Ted Williams moved away from the plate in order to punch the ball, he made sure he closed his stance in proportion to the distance he moved his back foot away.

As I mentioned, for the last seven or eight years, I haven't been hitting to my opposite field (right) at all. But the right-handed hitters I talk to who do hit to right will say you don't have to move your feet at all. The one adjustment they recommend is that, when you point your bat, instead of hitting down on the ball or swinging later, as some suggest, you try to push the ball off you. Swinging late sometimes has drawbacks. If you're a righty and you swing late, you may hit to right okay, but because the length of your swing is shortened you'll lose power. Also, there's a tendency when you swing late to swing under the ball and pop up. Contrary to common opinion, you can swing *early* and still punch the ball to right field (or to left if you're left-handed). The key to it is the pushing motion.

In the push swing, particularly on an outside pitch, your hands move ahead of the hitting end of the bat. Because the ball is hit late, the snap of your wrists is later than usual, and your hips move quickly but over a shorter distance. Some coaches advise hitters who have trouble hitting an outside pitch to the opposite field, to snap their wrists earlier as a way of bringing the bat into the ball at the same angle that would connect on an inside pitch. In this case the ball is hit later and the batter's body turns after the swing.

RIGHTIES, LEFTIES

People ask whether there's an advantage in hitting from one side of the plate or the other. A left-hand batter is two steps closer to first base. Aside from that it depends on what pitcher you're batting against. If it's somebody like a Sandy Koufax, or a Don Drysdale, Bob Gibson or Tom Seaver, you're better off to stay on the opposite side—and even that some-

Fig. 25

FIG. 25-27 When you try to hit to the "opposite" field (right field for a right-handed hitter), keep your hands ahead of the bat and push or punch the ball. Even in the follow-through your arms won't be fully extended. Your head and body will be facing right field.

Fig. 26

68   Fig. 27

times doesn't help. In other words, against a strong left-handed pitcher, you've got a better chance of hitting if you swing from the right side; against a righty, the left-handed hitter generally has the advantage, although a *good* hitter is going to get his share of hits regardless of whether a lefty or righty is on the mound. Ted Williams hit against both, so did Stan Musial—and look at Billy Williams!

I say this hitter-pitcher relationship is *generally* so, because of my own experience. I think I've done better against right-handed pitchers than against left-handers over the twenty years I've been in the majors. That's attributable to a couple of factors. Ever since I came to the Braves, we've been primarily a right-handed-hitting ball club and so our opponents, operating on the righty-pitcher versus righty-hitter supremacy theory, wouldn't throw many left-handers against us. Also, I tend to bear down harder against right-handers. I wait more. Almost three-quarters of my career home runs have been hit off righties.

But my case is exceptional. Generally speaking, the hitter who swings from the opposite side of the plate has the advantage. (Or, to state it from the hurler's viewpoint, a pitcher is usually more effective against a man who swings from the same side of the plate as he throws.)

There really isn't much you can do to compensate if, say, you're a right-handed hitter and you're facing a good right-handed pitcher. The main thing is to swing the way you always swing. Altering your style will probably hurt you more than it helps. Chances are you'll bear down a little more, concentrate more, if you're a righty hitter facing a righty pitcher. Be careful that it's not the opposite when you face a lefty. Overcome the tendency to relax and don't become overconfident.

SWITCH-HITTING

One way to escape the pitcher's advantage when you hit from the side he throws from is to be a switch hitter. Sometimes I think I should have been one. It would have kept me from facing right-handed ace Don Drysdale from the right side. Because of the way I started holding a bat —cross-handed—it probably would have been smart just to step to the other side of the plate and become a left-handed hitter (since my left hand was above my right on the bat). Switch-hitting was another logical alternative. But truthfully, if I had it to do over again, knowing that my career was going to be as successful as it is, I wouldn't have changed a thing.

69

If *you've* got the desire to become a switch hitter, by all means give hitting from either side of the plate a try. Don't wait until you're eighteen or nineteen. Start as early as you can, because if you can manage a bat either way you'll enjoy the benefit of not having to face those tough pitchers from the side where they have the advantage. You'll also be less likely to be "platooned," the (sometimes overdone) policy of managers' removing most of their right-handed hitters from the line-up when they're up against a righty pitcher.

So do try the switch-hitting idea young, if you think it's for you. Some experts are concerned that a young player trying to learn to hit from both sides of the plate will end up not doing it well from either. These observers say the player would be better off concentrating on getting better as a hitter from one side or the other. There's some truth in that, but the switch hitters I've seen have really concentrated on being equally dangerous from either side. Red Schoendienst, the only switch hitter I played with for any length of time, did fine. And it was certainly to Mickey Mantle's advantage to switch hit. So try it. You'll probably find you're a lot better one way. But if it turns out you can hit well from either side of the plate, you're that much ahead of the game.

4
Power Hitting

I suppose there's no getting around it: Hank Aaron is going to be remembered as a home-run hitter. Earlier I said I'd rather be remembered as a player who could do well in all baseball categories. As a hitter and baserunner, I consider that you're being helpful to your major-league team if you score a hundred runs in a season, bat in a hundred runs, hit .300 and steal 20 or 25 bases.

Saying this doesn't mean I don't enjoy hitting home runs. I *love* to hit them. To me, hitting a homer is the most exciting thing in baseball.

"Accidental" Homers

Believe it or not, of the more-than-700 home runs I've hit in my big-league career, I would say about 90 percent of them have come when I wasn't even thinking home run. I don't go up there with the idea that I can hit a homer anytime I get ready. If you go up to the plate just concentrating on hitting the ball hard, you'll naturally get your share of home runs (if you've got the power). That's often been the case with me; I was just concentrating on meeting the ball and was pleasantly surprised to hit the ball out.

Of course, there are times when I *try* to hit a homer. If I get up at bat in the ninth inning and we're behind by one run with nobody on, I know my job is to try to hit the ball out of the park. That would also be true if I came up in that situation in the seventh or eighth inning. If we're two runs behind, I know my job is to get on base. I'd try to get a rally started by getting on base, and help my team get runs that way.

One home run I'll always remember—it was one of the most exciting moments in my baseball career—clinched the 1957 National League pen-

71

nant for the Braves, whose hometown was then Milwaukee, in the eleventh inning. It came when I wasn't really thinking about hitting a home run.

Game circumstances will often dictate whether you should try to hit one out of the park. For instance, if there are two outs and nobody on and you're trailing by one run, it makes sense if you're a power hitter to try to park one, because otherwise, if you get a single say, it will take two more hits to drive in one run. You might also try for the distance if there are men on and your team is trailing by a lot.

The pitch I try to hit for a home run will also depend on circumstances. A 2-0 pitch, when the pitcher is likely to come in with the ball, might generally be a good one to try to hit into the stands. But again, if we're two runs behind and there's nobody on, I won't swing for it because I can't hit a two-run homer with no one on base. The pitcher will also be a factor. If the fellow out there has control, a Juan Marichal or Bob Gibson, for instance, I might swing on 2-0. (I once hit a homer on a 3-0 count off Bob.) But here too, even if I hit a home run we're still a run behind.

Some Myths

Many people believe that a home-run hitter has to be a pull hitter and built very large. Neither is necessarily so. You don't have to be a big bruiser, a musclebound 200-pounder, to hit a lot of homers. Dave Johnson, my teammate on the Braves, is 6'1" and weighs about 185 pounds, and when you look at him you don't think in terms of "slugger." Yet in 1973 he was second in the major leagues in home runs with 43.

I'm heavier now (189 pounds) than I was when I started out, but I hit a good number of homers when I weighed just 170 pounds. And I had better credentials with the bat then.

Compared to a Ted Kluszewski, whose arm muscles were so big he had to cut open his sleeves so his jersey would fit him, I'm not very big. But keep in mind that the power of your swing doesn't come entirely from your arms or shoulders. If your wrist action is strong and quick, you need only a relatively short swing to whack the ball hard and far.

Generally, though, it's true that maximum power from your swing will result when your bat travels through the greatest possible arc. When you pull the ball, you get ahead of the pitch, and if you're a right-handed hitter and the bat has gone through a big arc, the ball will be directed to left field. The reverse is true for a left-handed hitter. But you don't *have to* be a pull

72

hitter to get a good share of home runs. In my first few years in the big leagues, I suppose I hit as many home runs to right field as I did to left or center.

Knowing a Ball Is Gone

Often, after you've hit a lot of home runs, you'll know the instant you make contact that the ball is going over the fence.

(My 600th, for example, was off a high inside fastball by Gaylord Perry. I knew the moment I hit it that it was gone.) This is especially true in certain ballparks where the fences are closer than elsewhere. But whether you know when the ball leaves the bat, or if the home run is a complete surprise, it's a very pleasant feeling when it goes over.

Home-Run Pitches and Pitchers

Generally speaking, there's no particular pitch that's easier to hit out. Most sluggers prefer a pitch over the inside of the plate, belt-high or higher, because it's the easiest pitch to pull, and their great strength is on the side of the plate from which they bat. But it's possible to hit a low ball out of the park, too, if you manage to get enough bat on it. Or, for that matter, a fastball or curve ball. It depends on the type of hitter you are. If you're customarily a low-ball hitter, then that's the type you'll hit for a home run.

You'll find that some pitchers are very tough to hit home runs off. Yet there are surprises. Billy Muffett, whom I homered against to win the N.L. pennant in 1957, hadn't thrown a gopher to anyone in a long, long time. And Don Drysdale was one of the toughest pitchers I ever faced. Yet I hit more home runs against him than against any other pitcher in my career. And the first one off him was a grand slam.

It's an advantage for some pitchers to face a batter who they know is trying for a home run rather than just trying to meet the ball. Pat Dobson, who used to pitch for us, loved to see a man coming up there swinging for the fence. The reason is that Pat's the type of pitcher who can change speeds very well on everything he throws—his fastball, curve, slider, everything. And he throws just hard enough to keep a hitter off-balance. Pitchers probably throw extra cautiously to the long-ball hitter, so his work is cut out for him, particularly if he is overeager. They'll give him good pitches to hit only by accident, and tease him to death with pitches out of the strike zone.

73

As I got closer to the home-run record, there were stories about how some pitchers said they'd like to groove one for me to break the record. But I knew it was just talk. I hadn't seen a pitch deliberately thrown down the middle to me in twenty years, and I wasn't expecting to see one now. Any time I get a good pitch, I know I've worked hard to get it.

It is an advantage for most pitchers to face a man intent on hitting a home run. Yet with some pitchers it works just the opposite. Against these, especially those who always throw hard, batters who swing hard do very well.

Home-Run Hitters and Strikeouts

What you might call an "occupational hazard" for a home-run hitter is the strikeout—swinging or called. When you're swinging hard to overpower the ball you sacrifice some bat-control, compared with the player who's just trying to make contact. And this means you're going to miss the ball more often.

Also I know in my own case, when I'm looking for a home run in a close game, I may take two or three pitches looking for the one I can rip, and so I run the risk of being called out on strikes. (All in all, though, I think my strikeout total is about par for the number of homers I hit. And I don't strike out as much as some sluggers. Mickey Mantle, for instance, used to swing a lot harder than I do, and he struck out a lot more.)

Is it worth it? Well, home runs do save you and your team a lot of work. But on the other hand, trying for home runs has ruined or adversely affected the careers of players who should have been trying to meet, rather than kill, the ball. A lot of .220 or .230 hitters could add as much as 50 points to their batting averages if they stopped swinging for the fences. As an indication of how home runs can affect batting average, early in the 1973 season my batting average was embarrassing. I had only three hits in nine games, all of them homers. Then I got up to only ten base hits, five of them homers. Early in July I had just 54 hits, 23 of them home runs. As the season progressed, my hitting generally got a lot better, and at the end of the season, besides 40 home runs, my average was .301 and I had 96 runs batted in.

The important thing, obviously, is that you help your team win games. I hit my 600th against the San Francisco Giants, but Willie Mays' 10th-inning single beat us, 6-5. That spoiled my day. I hit my 700th when the Phillies beat us, 8-4. I'd rather have the team win.

How you can help the team the most depends, as we said, on your

74

capabilities and the circumstances. You might be a power hitter, but if the infield plays in you'll perform the best service by just meeting the ball to get it past the infielders rather than taking a big swing. There are hitters who swing from the heels on every pitch. The thinking hitter will know when not to swing too hard. There are hitters who can't adjust their swing even though they know they'll have more control over the shorter swing. But practice can overcome this.

Ideally, try to hit for distance without sacrificing bat-control. If you've got the capability, swing hard but not wildly. Even on a pitch that's just where you want it, try to be as quick as possible without losing control. This might mean holding back 10 or 15 percent of your full capacity. But it's better to do that than swing from the heels and miss. Give it all you've got with your hands, arms and wrists, but save a little in your shoulders and hips to keep from overswinging and losing your timing and possibly your balance.

I've always prided myself on my consistency as a hitter. Along with the home runs, I've averaged over .300, knocked in my share of runs, been on base a lot. (I have the record for extra-base hits.) I've never had a bad year. You needn't either, once you find out the kind of hitter you are and work accordingly. Never *press* for a home run—it will defeat your purpose. I never did, even with the pressure on to break Ruth's record. Incidentally, I didn't begin to think of myself as a home-run hitter until I was around a few years. When I was a rookie in 1954, we had Eddie Mathews and Joe Adcock for the long ball, and I considered myself just a guy who got on base. But when I got older and stronger, I also got more selective with the pitches I hit, and that turned into a home-run hitter. Then it was my responsibility. That same approach might be best for you.

5
What You're Up Against

Since the hitting battle narrows down to you and the pitcher, it might be worthwhile to examine briefly what a hitter is up against.

Control

A good pitcher knows how to throw strikes to spots, not strikes over the heart of the plate where a batter has an easy time hitting them, but over the corners, inside and outside, across the letters or the knees. If he's got control he'll not only know your weakness but be able to take advantage of it. You should know your weakness before he does and better than he does, and adjust your thinking accordingly. Be prepared for the pitch you have trouble with.

Good pitchers always throw the same type of stuff that they're out to make you hit. They're not going to serve up a mediocre fastball over the middle of the plate for you to hit; it's going to have something on it. Or they'll throw a good curve ball, not one that "hangs." These are the pitchers who win. Juan Marichal has a tremendous variety of pitches. He may throw you a screwball on the outside of the plate, a slider on the inside, a fastball on the inside. He has perhaps the most pitches of any pitcher I've seen in the big leagues—and he can control all of them.

VARIETY OF PITCHES

Let's take a look at the basic pitches the pitcher is likely to throw:

Fastball

The fastball is the pitch you'll see most often (even in the majors). This is the pitch that gets a lot of strikeouts. It isn't speed alone that makes a fastball effective. A good one doesn't come in flat, but, depending on how it is thrown, it will hop (or rise) as it crosses the plate, or sail, or tail off. If it sinks, it's likely to result in groundballs that can be turned into easy outs or double plays. It's the easiest pitch to control, but if it isn't fast enough or doesn't move enough, a fastball will really travel off your bat.

One reason I'll study a new pitcher and let some pitches go by is to find out how his fastball moves, whether it's coming in on me or away from me.

Sinker

A sinker is a pitch that—as you can tell from the name—breaks downward. It can be a natural variety of a fastball or slider that just naturally drops as it crosses the plate. Or it may be thrown so that it comes right at the batter and dips sharply.

Curve ball

The curve ball (which boys your age shouldn't be throwing) *does* curve. It can be thrown at varying speeds and angles of "break" from a straight line. A good curve is likely to come up to the plate like a fastball, but then will break down and away from a right-handed batter if thrown by a righty, and down and away from a left-hander if thrown by a southpaw.

Even though it's sometimes thrown at relatively fast speeds, a curve ball is slower than a fastball and you've got more time to hit it. If it doesn't break soon enough or far enough and "hangs," it can be hit with ease.

When I study a pitcher, one thing I look for is whether his curve is sharp enough and whether I've really got to concentrate on it.

Slider

A slider is a combination of fastball with something taken off it and a curve. It looks like a fastball as it nears the plate, but then it veers away to one side or the other. It has a downward slant, but not as sharp a slant as a curve.

A lot of homers are hit off sliders because if it doesn't slide it's about as effective as a fastball that isn't fast enough. But a lot of hitters have problems with it.

Knuckler

A knuckler is a slow breaking pitch that doesn't spin, and so it's affected by the least change in air currents or pressure. Hoyt Wilhelm could put it in the strike zone consistently, but generally it's a tough pitch to control—or catch—because nobody is certain just which way it will break. Because of its unpredictability, it's possibly the most difficult pitch to hit.

Screwball

A screwball, sometimes known as a scroogie, is a breaking pitch that will break away from a right-handed hitter when thrown by a lefty (the opposite action of a curve), and away from a left-handed hitter when thrown by a righty. It puts a strain on the pitcher's arm, and so it definitely isn't something a young boy should be throwing.

Change-of-Pace

A change-of-pace, also called a change-up, is a relatively slow pitch that contrasts with the speed of the fastball. It's thrown with the same motion that a pitcher uses to throw a fastball or curve. It's used to throw a hitter's timing off, especially a good fastball hitter. Just as a ground game sets up a pass in football, a change-up is effective for setting up a fastball, and vice versa. If you're not fooled by it, you can tag it. With a slow pitch, you're better off trying to meet the ball and hitting to the opposite field rather than taking a hard swing. This is especially true if it's low and outside.

Spitball

A spitball is an illegal pitch. Treated with saliva, perspiration or some other substance, the ball breaks with astounding and unexpected sharpness. But it's only as good as the pitcher throwing it. If he's good, it's hard to hit because you don't know which way it's going to break. The trouble is most pitchers don't know either, because they don't have control of it.

TOUGH PITCHES TO HIT

If you're not known to have a weakness, you've got a big advantage. I haven't had any problem hitting any of the standard pitches—sinker, slider, curve ball, screwball, or what have you. So it's difficult for me to identify the toughest pitch.

I would say the toughest *pitcher* is the one who keeps the hitter off stride. If a pitcher just goes out there and keeps throwing the same hard stuff, regardless of whether it's a breaking ball, hard slider or fastball, by the fourth or fifth inning the hitters will start timing the ball and hit it. The big thing the pitcher tries to do is keep the hitter off stride. To offset this, batters will do some educated guessing.

THE GUESSING GAME

Hitting is a great pleasure for me, but what I get the most enjoyment from is trying to outguess the pitcher and the catcher.

As the hitter, you're up at the plate by yourself, just you thinking for yourself at the moment, and it's a thrill to outguess two guys who are trying to outthink you. You don't guess wildly, but you take into consideration such things as the game situation, what the pitcher has been throwing, and what the count is on you. You can't expect the same pitch when the count is 0-2 as you would when it's 2-0, and you wouldn't look for a curve in a tough situation if a pitcher is getting only his fastball in the strike zone.

You also would consider what and how you and the pitcher have been doing against each other. For instance, late in the 1973 season I was batting against Ken Brett, the Philly left-hander. The first time I was up, he'd thrown me all breaking pitches, so this time I was halfway looking for a fastball. Sure enough, he came in with a low fastball, and I hit it out for my 700th career home run.

The guessing game goes back and forth between pitcher and hitter. A few seasons back, Claude Osteen of the Dodgers was pitching against us in a 3-3 game. He'd thrown me fastballs in two previous at-bats. This time he thought I'd be guessing fastball again, so he threw me a curve. I wasn't fooled, though, and I homered to break the tie.

Around the same time we faced Dave Roberts, then pitching for the San Diego Padres, and it was 1-1 in the ninth. I had seen two left-handers in two nights prior to that game and I hadn't had a hit off either one. It was getting kind of embarrassing. Now Roberts was giving me a fit. I couldn't figure him out. He was throwing everything for strikes. Finally, I guessed fastball and that's what came in. It wasn't too high, but Roberts, a heck of a

79

pitcher, probably wanted to get it farther away. I hit it out for a two-run homer and we won, 3-1.

But don't get the impression that major-league hitters are constantly guessing right. Even the best guessers sometimes outguess themselves. I know how guessing can cost a hitter.

On the last day of the 1973 season we were facing the Houston Astros and it was Dave Roberts starting for them. My first time up he used reverse psychology on me. I was sure he'd give me the change-up, but he threw a fastball right down the middle for a called strike. It was the only good pitch he gave me, the only strike. Eventually he threw me a slow slider that I managed to top for an infield single.

In the fourth inning he jammed me inside, but I knew I wasn't going to get anything better, so I swung. The ball blooped off my bat into center for another single. And in the sixth the same thing happened. Another inside pitch and another single, my third of the day.

Then my last time up, in the bottom of the eighth, with everyone yelling for me to hit home run number 714 to tie Ruth's record, reliever Don Wilson jammed me on the fists with a fastball. It was a bad pitch but I'd been guessing, so I swung anyway and all I got was a soft pop to the second baseman.

To a certain extent every hitter guesses, and as one observer has pointed out, if he's right he was "thinking"; if he's wrong he was "guessing." What this means, essentially, is that the batter anticipates the type, speed and location of the pitch that is coming next. Naturally what happened your last time at bat is going to be a factor. If the pitcher had you swinging and missing on an inside curve, will he come back with the same pitch? Or will he throw a fastball? Or a change-up? And, if so, will it be inside or out, high or low? If you're right often enough, you'll have a fine batting average and be called a genius. If you're wrong, well . . .

Many batting theories recommend that the hitter assume every pitch is going to be a fastball. But others say it's better—at least in the case of straight-away or opposite-field hitters—to anticipate a medium-speed pitch. Often this will depend on what a given pitcher is known to throw regularly. With some fastball hurlers, it isn't enough to anticipate a fastball; you've got to get out in front of it.

Some believe that if you have a problem with a particular pitch, that's what you should always anticipate. Then there's the feeling that you should invariably guess curve or fastball, but swing only if the pitcher throws what you expected. This is something you can't do, of course, with two strikes on you.

It's really not enough for a hitter to guess. He's got to have the self-control to take a pitch outside the strike zone, or a strike on a type of pitch or in a spot that gives him trouble. Then, when he guesses correctly on a favorite pitch, he can give the ball a good ride.

DON'T YOU GUESS

Having said all this—and as pleasurable as outguessing the opposition can be—I don't recommend it for you at this stage of your game. Instead of guessing, concentrate on being quick with the bat and making your hands a lot quicker, and try to develop your hitting form. In other words, learn the fundamentals rather than try to guess whether it's going to be a curve, fastball, slider or screwball.

The reason I say this is that if you start thinking *too much* at the plate—and this has happened to me—the first thing you know you're outthinking yourself. And that can cause its own problems, especially if you don't have your fundamentals down pat. The ability to predict different types of pitches will automatically come once you've established yourself as a professional baseball player.

By the same token, I don't think it's helpful to have signs stolen for you when you're up at the plate. Not at your age. I think you should hit on your own. I've stolen signs and flashed them to batters on my club, but I've never been able to take a sign from a coach or one of our players and been able to hit the ball. I find it's like trying to sock a 3-0 pitch. Even though a guy's going to throw it right down the middle, you usually can't do it.

So I think you should hit on your own. Develop your mind so that you think on your own while at the plate rather than have someone do it for you. And there's another very practical reason for relying on your own judgment: Miss one time and duck your head into a fastball, and it's all over.

LOCATION OF PITCHES

In general, no matter what type of pitch is thrown to you and whatever its location, a very hard swing is likely to upset your timing. You're better off using a medium-hard swing and depending on the strength of your wrists and hands for a lot of your power. Wrists were an important part of Willie Mays' hitting success, to name one outstanding example. A wrist hitter has more time to see what kind of pitch is coming in, and where it is—inside or out, high or low.

Whether or not you're a wrist hitter, there are some basic points that can be helpful in handling pitches in particular locations.

Inside Pitch

On an inside pitch it's important that you get your hips out of the way, rolling them around to do it. Also, make sure that you get the head of the bat out in front rather than wait for the ball to come right up on you. If you're normally a pull hitter, a push swing can help you go to the opposite field, even on an inside pitch.

Outside Pitch

To hit an outside pitch your arms should be extended, but your hips shouldn't roll. If you can control the roll you can hit to the opposite field with a lot of power. Hitters like Willie Mays, who had tremendous power to all fields, resist the temptation of some pull hitters to lunge at the ball or stride too quickly. Ernie Banks had the ability to *pull* an outside pitch. Bat speed was probably the key ingredient. You should concentrate on making good contact and hitting the ball where it's pitched.

High Pitch

To hit a high pitch you can't have any upswing in your bat at all. And again, make sure your arms are away from your body, and be sure to get ahead with your bat. Hit the ball out in front so it will carry out.

Low Pitch

Many pitchers in our league throw sinkers and other low pitches. The only way you're going to be able to handle these is to bend your knees slightly. The tendency is to hit a low ball on the ground, but if you bend your knees and go down with the pitch, you'll be able to make up for the low altitude.

I used to have a lot of trouble with low pitches until I began getting down with the ball where I could see it well. And I waited longer and made sure my arms were away from my body.

82

At this stage, *I* can't change my way of swinging and hit to my full potential. But *you* can if you feel comfortable doing it. Possibly move up on the plate a bit and try to punch the ball to the opposite field. But, all in all, you're better off staying with and concentrating on what you can do best.

EARLY, LATE

If you're grounding out a lot, you're probably swinging too early. This most likely means you're getting fooled on pitches or that you're *too far* out in front to hit the ball solidly. Adjust accordingly. If you're popping up a lot, you're probably swinging late and getting under the ball. It's not too bad being late with your swing, *if* you're real quick with your bat.

THE COUNT

As we've mentioned, the balls-and-strikes count on you is going to have a lot to do with what the pitcher throws and what you can hit. Let's discuss those factors in detail.

Behind the Pitcher
Strikeouts are frustrating. How to avoid them? If you're behind the pitcher with, let's say, an 0-2 count, the main thing you should concentrate on is not swinging at a bad pitch.

I don't think you should adjust anything in the way of "guarding" the plate by trying to get closer to it, or moving forward in the batter's box, slightly widening your stance, gripping the bat a trifle higher or adjusting your swing. You have enough of a problem just concentrating on the strike zone rather than moving from your customary position.

Of course, there are going to be balls outside the strike zone that are too close for comfort. You can't afford the luxury of letting those go by. Possibly you'll foul them off.

Sometimes you'll see hitters with two strikes on them foul off one pitch after another. I wish I could deliberately foul off a ball, but I can't. I've seen some hitters who could. Richie Ashburn was one good example. I think the main reason he was capable of doing this was that he was a punch hitter rather than a home-run hitter—he'd hit four or five a year, if that

83

many—but he concentrated on hitting the ball where it was pitched. If he was looking for the ball away from him and the pitch came in on the inside, he could foul it off deliberately.

One reason there are so many fouls hit on two-strike pitches is that the hitter is probably chopping at pitches he might have taken with less than two strikes. Up until the count reached that point, the batter could be picky. But now that there are two strikes, it's the pitcher who has the advantage on him, and he's got to protect against a called third strike. So he can't afford to let pitches that are too close to the strike zone go by. And he's got to be quicker.

A way that some suggest to protect the plate—and yourself—is to choke up on the bat, to shorten your swing and give you better control. The push swing, the one you'd use to hit to the opposite field, is ideal in this situation, they say, because by shortening your bat and becoming quicker you can wait longer and you're less likely to be fooled by a pitch.

But beware that adjusting your swing doesn't cost you in terms of lessened concentration on the strike zone.

Ahead of the Pitcher

If you're ahead of the pitcher on the count, you can be a little more choosy about what you swing at. If you're fooled on a given pitch, you can take it with less than two strikes. And you stand a better chance of getting a pitch you like because the pitcher, in danger of issuing a walk, will have to come in with the pitch. On a 2-0 or 3-1 count, when the pitcher is likely to come over the plate with the ball, you can try to give the ball a long ride.

When you have the pitcher in a hole at 3-0, your coach might give you the go-ahead to swing at the next pitch and try to drive it out. This is fine if, say, the pitcher grooves the fastball. But some pitchers do their best work when they're behind. Warren Spahn, the great left-hander recently inducted into the Hall of Fame, was a teammate of mine. I remember how he used to love to pitch when he was behind the batter. As everyone around the league knew—or soon found out—he had such good control that when he'd get behind, two balls and no strikes, he'd make the batter bite on a bad screwball.

I've hit maybe five home runs off a 3-0 pitch. One I mentioned earlier came in 1972 off Bob Gibson. Usually the batter doesn't swing on that count, but my manager at the time, Luman Harris, gave me the green light to swing. This was about the third inning and I guessed he'd throw me a

84

fastball down the middle, probably figuring it was an automatic "take" situation. Just trying to put it down, he did throw one. You've got to take advantage of Gibby when he throws one like that. The longer he works, the sharper he gets, and I knew I might never see another one like that the rest of the game—and maybe the rest of my life. So I swung and hit a home run.

But that's an exceptional situation. A number of other times I've had the green light to swing on 3-0, counts, but either I tried to hit the ball too hard, or, knowing exactly what was coming, I'd swing at a bad pitch. So I'd rather hit a 3-2 or 3-1 pitch, when I'm concentrating on meeting the ball, rather than try to hit when I'm far ahead on the count and knowing that a fastball is coming. More than half my career home runs have come on 3-1 or 3-2 counts.

Whether you're behind the count or ahead, you've got to concentrate on not swinging at a bad pitch.

SWINGING AT THE FIRST PITCH

You may read that sometimes a team will begin swinging at the first pitch, but I don't think it's an advantage. If you're hitting against a Gibson or Seaver or some of the other pitchers who have been around for some time and know the strike zone, if you guess fastball and are lucky enough to get it, swing. But if the hurler has his stuff, he's going to be tough on the first, second or last pitch—so it really isn't an advantage.

If fact, some feel it might pay to *take* the first pitch to remind yourself of the pitcher's speed and delivery and to see what kind of stuff he has that day. In fact, they advise making that first time at bat a learning experience. As for myself, whether or not I swing at first pitches seems to go in cycles. For a week I may swing at them. Other times I won't.

My advice to you is to remember what we said when we talked about waiting. Too much waiting can be self-defeating. If you get the kind of pitch you want in the strike zone, swing at it whether it's the first or second pitch or whatever. You may not get a better one to swing at.

HITTING THE FIRST STRIKE

So I'm emphasizing again that you can't really afford the luxury of letting a good pitch go by. There are times when it's really important that you swing at the first good strike—for instance, when there is a runner or runners on base and a score will make the game close or tie it up or put your team ahead. Another example is in a normal sacrifice situation where the infielders are probably out of position and you've got a good chance of hitting the ball safely.

If your team is far behind or the pitcher is wild, you can afford to wait out the pitcher. Similarly, when first base is open and you're not the potential winning or tying run, you're better off not swinging at a questionable pitch. Since in those circumstances a walk isn't likely to be damaging, the pitcher will often try to pitch every ball to the batter's weakness. So being overanxious will particularly hurt you.

Making a pitcher throw a lot gets him tired, which is to your team's advantage, but in your league you shouldn't let a *good* pitch go by for that reason alone.

I've found that as I grow older I get a bit more patient in waiting for a good pitch. At *any* age, be patient, but not so much that you let a good hitting opportunity go by.

6
Strategy

Baseball is a very strategic game—full of plotting and counterplotting to gain an advantage that might result in winning a ballgame. Your coach or manager will make the strategic decisions for your team. Here are some of the principles involved.

BATTING ORDER

There are many factors in baseball strategy. Your particular responsibilities in carrying out the strategy will sometimes depend on where you are hitting in the line-up, and this is a matter for your manager or coach to decide. It will benefit you to know the general responsibilities of each hitter according to his slot in the order.

The *lead-off man* has to be capable of getting on base often. This means he has to get a lot of base hits and have a good enough eye to draw a lot of walks. People like Ron Hunt are even willing to get on base by letting themselves get hit by pitched balls.

There is some feeling that clubs should put a stronger hitter up first so that he might get an extra turn at bat during the game. In general, I don't agree, although it depends primarily on what the man can do. San Francisco has Bobby Bonds, a very good hitter, up first. He strikes out a lot, especially for a lead-off man, but he gets on base maybe 200 times a season and steals a lot of bases. (A lead-off man should have excellent speed and be a good baserunner.) Bobby usually gets on base once or twice a game, and he has the ability to come up with the home run.

The *second-place hitter* in the line-up is the man able to handle the bat, hit behind the runner, execute hit-and-run plays, bunt a runner to scoring position. In other words, the second-place hitter is capable of getting the bat on the ball and not striking out much. A hitter like Joe Morgan of the Cincinnati Reds, who hits second, could be a good lead-off man, too. He walks a great number of times. Pete Rose, the Most Valuable Player in the National League in 1973, who leads off for the Reds, doesn't walk as much as Joe but does more things. He's more aggressive at the plate, gets 200 hits a year, so I think manager Sparky Anderson is wise in using Joe behind Pete in the line-up.

You might say that from second to fifth in the batting order is where you're going to win ballgames. When I was first assigned to the number-three spot I felt very proud of the responsibility. The *third-place hitter* is often the best hitter on the team, combining power with a high batting average. If the first- and second-place hitters are carrying out their responsibilities, there should be a man on base for him to drive in, and he should knock in a hundred runs a year. And if he's got anybody at all hitting after him, he should score that many runs, as well as hit .300 or close to it. He's got to be a fearsome hitter, capable of both hitting the long ball and getting on base. And he should not strike out much.

Your *fourth-* and *fifth-place* batters are basically the same type of hitters as the man who bats third, although they may strike out more. But they give you power and drive in over a hundred runs a year. The fourth-place batter is a home-run hitter. He's known as the "clean-up" hitter because if there are men on base it's expected—or hoped—he'll clean up the bases with a homer.

The *sixth-place hitter*, also well thought of by his manager, is also expected to hit with power, although he may not have as good a batting average as the men preceding him.

The weakest hitters on the team—often the shortstop and the catcher, and always the pitcher—hit in the seventh, eighth and ninth positions. Johnny Bench, of course, is a catcher who's a powerful exception to this. (As you probably know, American League teams are allowed to pinch-hit for one hitter, almost always the pitcher, throughout the game, without the team having to remove the player he pinch-hit for from the game. The pinch-hitter can keep coming up in that role, without having to take the field.)

The hitters at the bottom of the batting order have an added disadvantage (except where the designated hitter is used). In addition to their own hitting problems, they're hitting in front of the team's worst hitter, which means an opposing pitcher may bear down extra hard to get them out, so he can face their pitcher, a "sure" out, to start the next inning.

No matter where in the line-up you bat, there are certain plays that you should know how to execute.

BUNTING

During the 1973 season, when I was closing in on the home-run record, my usual mission was to swing away—if not for a homer, at least to give the ball a good ride. So it was quite a surprise for me in one close game to have a bunt sign flashed to me. We had a runner on first, and my job was to bunt him over to second.

I tried, but wasn't successful. Part of the problem may have been that I was out of practice, because bunting successfully does require practice. When I was much younger I used to bunt a lot, but since I hadn't bunted in many years I'd lost all my concentration. If I'd kept bunting all through my career, it wouldn't have been any problem to sacrifice my teammate along. As a matter of fact, I should be able to bunt a man over more easily than someone else, because when I'm at bat they're not anticipating a bunt and consequently they're not going to be ready to charge in.

Here I am bunting for a base hit. I believe a player, slugger or otherwise, should be willing to do anything he can to help his team win.

WIDE WORLD PHOTOS

89

People ask me if a slugging star gets insulted when he's asked to bunt. Well, I was surprised that day, but I certainly wasn't insulted. My main purpose is to try to win games. A couple of seasons ago I told a writer that if a bunt would win a game or a pennant on the last day of the season and I had 713 home runs, I'd still bunt. I meant it. I've been on a couple of pennant-winning ballclubs and I know the prestige that goes along with it, so I'd do most anything to try and win—and that includes bunting.

And I'm not the only one who feels that way. Leading off in the second inning of the fourth game of the 1973 National League playoff, Johnny Bench, one of the leading sluggers in baseball, who'd won the opening contest with a ninth-inning homer, tried to bunt his way on. It was worth a try because Johnny's team, the Reds, hadn't been hitting against the Mets, and the surprise element was in his favor to get a rally going. He was out on a close play.

No matter how good or powerful a hitter you are, you should know how to bunt. It's a neglected side of the game, and it shouldn't be. A good bunt can tie games, even win them. It takes practice. Some pitchers in our organization spend hours in the batting cage trying to teach themselves to bunt. Not only pitchers or second-place hitters should learn to bunt. *Everyone* can profit from this ability.

What you do physically to execute a bunt will depend on the intent of your bunt. Basically, bunts have one of two purposes: either to move one or two of your teammates farther along the base paths, or to get a base hit. Let's look at them in detail.

SACRIFICE BUNTS

When you sacrifice in baseball it means you've given up a chance of a base hit for yourself in order to move a teammate farther along the base paths. When you're willing to make out so that the other man can get closer to scoring a run, you probably don't care who else knows what your intention is.

Most likely the other team is expecting your bunt anyway—since certain situations, such as a man on first and none out, and your team a run behind, cry out for a bunt. So the opposing first and third basemen will be charging in, and then you might as well square around to bunt, not make any attempt to hide it. Getting into bunting position quickly will give you a better chance of executing a successful sacrifice.

Usually when a sacrifice is your intention, and you're in position, you can wait for a pitch you can bunt well. (A pitcher expecting a batter to bunt will probably throw high and inside, hoping he pops up.) The only thing you have to concentrate on is getting your bat on the ball in such a way that you deaden the ball. This prevents it from rolling so hard to either the first baseman, third baseman or pitcher that he can throw your teammate out on the bases.

Rather than swing, you almost "catch" the ball with your bat. In other words, there's no wrist action at all. You just hold the bat and let the ball hit it. You don't push, unless you know the opposing first or third baseman is not a good fielder and you want to make sure he fields it. But otherwise, you merely want to deaden the ball so that by the time it's fielded, the only play is to first base and the runner advances to scoring position (or if a man was already on second, he makes it safely to third).

Bunting Position

Start by taking your normal hitting position in the box. It's recommended that you stand fairly tall because of the likelihood that the pitcher will throw high and fast in a sacrifice situation.

As the pitcher goes into his delivery, square around so that you're facing him from head to toe. There are a couple of ways you can accomplish this maneuver. Either swing (pivot) around on your front foot and bring your back foot up parallel with it—or, if you normally stand very close to the plate, pivot on your back foot and bring your front foot back on a line with the back foot. There are players who move both feet; they bring the front foot away from the plate and the back foot up even with it.

In any case, as the pitcher delivers, swing around so you're facing him. Preferably stand toward the front of the batter's box. Your weight should be evenly distributed on the balls of your feet with your legs spread comfortably apart. Bend slightly at the waist and knees. Don't delay getting into this position or you may find the bat is moving forward as you bunt, and the ball will probably get to an infielder too soon for the sacrifice to work.

The Bat

As you pivot around toward the pitcher, your upper hand should move up to about the trademark of the bat, while your lower hand stays where it was. The bottom hand, which controls the direction of the bat, grips it firmly, while the bat rests lightly either on the fingertips of your upper hand, or on its fingers, with the thumb on top. Don't let the fingers curl around the bat where they can be struck by the pitch.

The Chicago Cubs hold the bat diagonally in most bunting situations, with the barrel up around the shoulder and the handle down at waist-level. But the most common stance is to hold the bat roughly parallel to the ground with elbows slightly bent and the bat out where you can see it. In fact, you should actually see the ball hitting the bat.

It's a good idea to hold the bat around the top of your strike zone, because of the likelihood of a high pitch. If the pitch comes in low, you can bend your knees to meet it.

Hold the bat still and let the ball hit it—don't start running to first base until the ball and bat have made contact.

When to Bunt

A sacrifice bunt is usually tried when there is a man on first or second base, or both, and none out. A weak hitter might be instructed to bunt with one out. In any case, a sacrifice is seldom tried with two strikes because if you should foul the ball off, it's strike three—as if you'd missed the pitch entirely. There are times, however, mainly in the case of a weak hitter, when the bunt is attempted even with two strikes. The thinking here is that if he fouls it off, a strikeout is still better than a double play.

Where to Bunt

Since a pitcher who expects a bunt will probably try to pitch high and inside, it's recommended, as mentioned earlier, that you stand fairly upright. Try to bunt on top of the ball. It's generally easier for a left-handed batter to bunt this kind of pitch down the third-base side, and a righty hitter to the first-base side. The position of the infielders might make you change your thinking—and the direction of your bunt.

If there's a runner on first, you should try to bunt the ball slowly between the pitcher's mound and one of the baselines. The first-base side is good in this situation, because the first baseman will usually stay on the base until the pitcher starts his delivery. Try to avoid bunting the ball hard along the third-base line because it could result in a double play.

If you're trying to sacrifice a runner from second to third base, try to

FIG. 28 To bunt for a sacrifice, run your upper hand near the label of the bat, pivot so that you face the pitcher in a slight crouch, and let the ball hit the bat.

bunt the ball fairly hard along the third-base line past the pitcher so that the third baseman will have to field it and leave the bag uncovered. If there's a runner on second and no one on first, you might try a bunt down the first-base line, since the runner going into third would have to be tagged. These are just a few possible situations, the strategy for which might change according to a variety of conditions, including your bunting ability.

Faking a Bunt

When you know a runner is going to attempt a steal, you can fake a bunt to help him. You get into the bunt position and, although you take the pitch, the infielders will probably be drawn out of position and your teammate will be helped to steal the base. If you perform your fake from the back of the batter's box, it might affect the catcher's handling of the ball.

BUNTING FOR A HIT

There will be times when you want to bunt for a base hit. Unlike a sacrifice bunt, when masking your intention isn't vital, in bunting for a hit the element of surprise is a big factor. So hold your normal batting stance and delay as long as possible giving away your intention. At the last possible instant, whip into position and bunt the ball *as you start moving toward first base.*

Drag Bunts

The usual technique used in bunting for a hit is the *drag bunt*, in which you drag the ball with the bat as you run toward first.

I have seen some right-handed batters do this, but for the most part a drag bunt is executed by left-handed hitters, who have a couple of steps' head-start toward first.

You should hold your bat parallel to the ground at about hip-level, almost behind you, and carry the bat as if you're going to run all the way to first with it.

A fastball is the best pitch to drag. A curve ball is tough, especially if it's thrown by a left-handed pitcher away from a left-handed batter.

As you drag bunt, you lean your weight forward onto your front foot

94

while keeping your arms back at the hip. The best time to drag, of course, is when the first baseman is playing deep. Then you try to drag the ball past the pitcher but in too far for the first baseman to make a play in time.

Push Bunt, Dump Bunt

Right-handed hitters trying to bunt their way on will generally *push* or *dump* the ball. When the first baseman is playing deep, a righty hitter will push the ball down the first-base line just hard enough so that the pitcher won't be able to field it. By the time the first or second baseman gets to the ball and the pitcher covers first and the throw is made—all requiring perfect timing—you should be on base. This depends a lot, of course, on how well you disguised your intention, how well you placed the ball and how fast you are.

You may also choose to dump the ball down the third-base line. This is a good tactic when the third baseman is slow or playing deep and when the pitcher is not good at fielding bunts. You can dump it short or try to put it beyond the pitcher's reach. In either case you bunt the ball while on the move.

Fingers, Arms, Hands

In the push bunt, you hold the bat with a little more tenseness in your fingers, wrists and arms than when you're bunting to sacrifice or bunting short for a base hit. Your top hand should have a firm grasp of the bat so you can push it sharply. To execute a push bunt, extend your arms in the direction of where you're bunting the ball.

Feet

If you're a lefty about to try a drag bunt, pivot on the ball of your right foot and take a crossover step with the left. This has the effect of a running start. If you're a righty, some suggest that you slide your rear foot back as the pitcher starts his wind-up to give yourself that running start.

When to Bunt for a Hit

Usually, no signal is given to the batter to try to bunt his way on. If you're trying it on your own, remember some of the dangers: If you try it with two strikes on you and you foul the ball off, you've struck out. Trying to bunt your way on when there are two outs will certainly surprise the opposition (and probably your own team as well), but it isn't smart to try it unless there's no one on base and your team is either ahead, tied or no more than a run behind. It makes sense with two outs if you're capable of stealing a base or a power hitter follows you in the line-up.

Faking a Bunt

It's a good idea to fake a bunt every once in a while to draw the first and third basemen in. Then you've got a better chance of a base hit in their direction.

SQUEEZE PLAYS

One of the most exciting—and dangerous—uses of the bunt is in the *squeeze play*. The squeeze play is a surprise tactic in which the batter tries to score a runner from third with a bunt. There are two types—the *suicide* and the *safety*.

Suicide Squeeze

In the suicide squeeze, the runner on third breaks for home as the pitcher is about to release the pitch. There's no turning back, and if the batter fails to make contact with the ball, that runner is a dead duck. That's where the term "suicide" comes into the picture.

So when you're the batter and the third-base coach flashes you the squeeze sign, you know you've *got* to bunt that next pitch, no matter where it is. Even if it's over your head or in the dirt you've got to get some wood on it, because the runner is charging down the line with the pitch, and his life as a runner is worthless if the catcher is holding the ball waiting for him.

Surprise

Obviously, the suicide squeeze depends on surprise. And because you don't want to alert your opponents to your intention until the last split-second, you can't afford to pivot. That would be a dead giveaway. So when the pitcher's getting ready to release the ball and the runner is preparing to break for home, keep your normal batting stance. Then, with the pitch near the plate, just flip your wrist, top hand over, to bunt the ball. Actually you don't even have to do that, just so long as you make sure you manage to bunt. And you can do that the same way that you execute the sacrifice bunt, only this time without pivoting. Run your top hand up on the bat and keep your fingers out of the way of the ball at the front of the bat.

Gamble

The suicide squeeze is a big gamble because a lot of things have to go just right. If your opponents anticipate that you're going to try a squeeze, they'll pitch out and maybe pick the runner off.

The play generally is tried only if the run will tie the game or put your team a run ahead, or add to a small lead that your team enjoys. It should be tried when the pitcher is likely to come in with a good pitch, and so, if your coach or manager is smart, he'll call the play when you, the batter, are ahead of the pitcher.

If everything works, even a slow runner can score on a suicide squeeze. It's a big gamble, yes, but it's worth it if it succeeds.

Safety Squeeze

Nine times out of ten, when a bunt is called for with a runner on third, it's a suicide squeeze. Occasionally, though, what's called for is a *safety* squeeze rather than a suicide. In a safety—as you might guess from the name—the runner on third plays it safe. Instead of starting to dash home with the pitch—do or die—he waits to see whether the batter is successful in bunting.

Has to Be Good

The safety squeeze differs from the suicide, in which almost any kind of bunt will score the runner because he broke for the plate as the pitcher released the ball. It requires a very well-placed bunt and is employed when either the first or third baseman plays back.

Again, surprise is a factor, but since the runner is playing it safe the batter can wait until he gets a pitch he feels he can bunt well. It's up to the runner to be alert to the possibility of a safety bunt. If it's well-executed he

97

should be able to beat the throw to the plate.

It helps, of course, if the runner is speedy, but if your bunt is good enough, even a slow runner might be able to score.

When Used

Sometimes a safety squeeze is tried with runners on first and third, just to prevent a pitcher or another weak hitter from hitting into a double play. The man on first breaks for second, but the runner on third stays put unless the bunt is particularly well-placed, or the other team tries for a double play.

Look for Signals

It's important to look to your third-base coach for a signal whenever you're at bat. If you look to him only when you think a squeeze or some other play is likely, it will tip off your opponents. On the other hand, if you look to him every time up, even when nothing is in the wind, they won't be alerted to anything special when something is really on.

SACRIFICE FLY

When there are less than two outs and you've got a man on third, often all you want to do is hit a fly ball on which he can tag up and come in to score. As far as I know, there's no surefire technique to get the ball high and deep enough to get him in. Hitting a sacrifice fly comes, I think, from concentration—just concentrating on hitting that ball solidly. Basically, when I'm trying to hit a sacrifice fly, I'll stand the same way and swing the same way as always. I don't believe in changing my swing or stance to do certain things, because once I make a change, I'm going to get into a slump and have to readjust my whole thinking—and my swing.

Avoid Hitting Grounders

When there's a runner on base and you're hitting away, you obviously want to avoid hitting into a double play. Ground balls are usually the culprits, but unfortunately I don't think there's a foolproof way to avoid hitting the ball on the ground. Against a sinkerball pitcher, for instance,

98

probably 90 percent of the balls hit off him will be grounders. I've gone weeks and weeks at a time without being able to hit a ball in the air. Then, too, I've gone weeks when I wasn't able to hit a ball on the ground. Once more, it's a matter of concentrating to hit the ball squarely.

HITTING BEHIND THE RUNNER

One often-used technique to avoid hitting into a double play is to hit behind the runner on first. This means that you attempt to hit the ball toward the opening between the second baseman and the first baseman, who ordinarily will be very close to the first-base bag, since he holds the base against the runner until the pitcher throws.

If you manage to hit the ball hard, there's a good chance it will go into the outfield for a base hit. In this case the runner has a good chance of making it safely to third base. If the ball is fielded (probably by the second baseman going to his left), the chance of a force play at second is less likely. That is, if you've placed it properly.

You might want to hit to right, even when there are men on first and second and the first baseman is not holding the bag. Chances of a force play at second are greater, but a double play isn't very likely. If you were up with none out, there would now be runners on first and third with only one out.

Left-handed batters have a natural advantage of hitting behind the runner, since they usually hit to right field. Inside pitches are generally best for a lefty trying to hit to right. Right-handed hitters have to push the pitch, preferably an outside one, to right field. When hitting behind the runner is likely, a pitcher may deliberately pitch inside to a righty and outside to a lefty to make the objective more difficult to accomplish. Some righties back up slightly from the plate in order to hit an inside pitch to right. Swinging down helps the ball travel on the ground.

HIT-AND-RUN

One of baseball's basic hitting plays is the *hit-and-run*. What it consists of is the runner on first breaking for second as the pitcher goes into his motion, with the batter trying his best to hit the ball—either behind the runner or through any hole left by the infielder who comes over to cover second.

The latter is the picture play. Let's suppose you're a left-handed hitter. There's a man on first and the hit-and-run is called for. The pitcher starts his motion and your teammate dashes for second. Because you're a left-handed batter and normally hit to the right side of the infield, the shortstop will probably cover second against what is treated as an attempted steal. You then proceed to punch the pitch through the spot where the shortstop had been before he moved to cover second. With a good jump the runner might make it safely to third.

As beautiful as that is to see, and for the player to execute, one main objective of the hit-and-run is to avoid a double play. Even if you hit the ball on the ground where it can be fielded, the fact that the runner has started with the pitch considerably cuts the chance of a play for him at second. It's very important once the runner has broken for you to swing at the pitch to protect him. There are times, for instance, when the catcher suspects a hit-and-run or steal attempt is in the making and calls for a pitchout. You've got to try to get a piece of the ball, even if it means lunging at an outside pitch and fouling it off.

A line drive to the infield will probably result in an easy double play, but that's the gamble—or at least one of the gambles—with the hit-and-run. The rewards make the gamble worthwhile.

When to Try It

Your coach or manager will probably call for the hit-and-run play only when there's a man on first and when your team is ahead or close behind. As with the squeeze play, it's usually called for when the pitcher is behind on the count and has to get the ball over. When the count is 3-1 or 3-2, you don't have to swing at a wide pitch to protect the runner since, obviously, that will be ball four and he'll make it to second safely. The play will usually be called when there are less than two outs, but as with most things, a lot of factors will determine the decision, such as the score, how far along the game is and what kind of batter you are.

Once in a while, the hit-and-run may be ordered when there's a runner on second. When he breaks, the third baseman has to go over to cover third, and that leaves a nice hole for a batsman to aim for, especially a righty.

100

When you're swinging at a wide pitch to protect the runner, don't concern yourself with where to hit it. Just make contact. Also, you can't always count on a particular infielder (the shortstop or second baseman) covering second when the runner breaks, especially if you're a hitter who is known to hit to all fields.

Always watch for your coach's sign.

DRAWING WALKS

I don't think there's any particular way to draw a walk, except to be careful as a hitter. A lot depends on who's batting behind you. If you're a hitter who's feared and the man hitting after you is not a great threat, you may get intentional walks. If he's a good hitter, they're less likely to pitch around you. When pitchers find out you're not going to go after bad balls, they either have to pitch around you or give you something better to hit.

I don't like to be walked, but there's not much I can do about it. If they come, they come, but I don't look for walks, because it might mean taking balls that are an inch off the plate that I could hit out of the ballpark. I don't go up with the idea of taking; I believe in being an aggressive hitter. The Pittsburgh Pirates are an aggressive ballclub. They go up there with one thing in mind—swinging the bat. They know if you don't do that, you're not going to hit.

This doesn't mean you should swing at bad balls just to avoid being walked. Remember that a run scored by a man who walks counts just as much as one by the man who singled. So look the pitches over carefully, and don't swing until there's a good one in your strike zone.

101

7

Conditioning and Practice

The player who is in better shape is going to play better baseball. The fellow who's strong, rested and tuned-up is going to do everything well—including hitting—and he's going to be able to withstand the rigors of a long season.

Accordingly, as far as I'm concerned, playing baseball is a twelve-month job. Even when the playing season is over, you've got to work at staying in shape.

Weight: Sluggers Can't Be Sluggish

I broke into the starting line-up with the Braves as a rookie partly because another player was out of shape. I'd played winter ball to get outfield experience and was in top shape, but Jim Pendleton had reported to spring training in 1954 about twenty pounds overweight and the Braves' manager at the time, Charlie Grimm, wanted him to work himself into form. Meanwhile, Grimm got a chance to see what I could do against major-league pitching, and when Bobby Thomson, our regular leftfielder, broke a leg sliding in spring training, it was me, not Pendleton, who replaced Bobby in the regular line-up.

Weight is an ever-present danger for a ballplayer. I've seen an awful lot of players who had a good year and then, first thing you know, they're out on the banquet circuit filling up on things like chicken and potatoes. By the time spring training rolls around they're maybe fifteen or twenty pounds over their ideal playing weight. They may think they're going to lose it all in six weeks of spring training, but they can't. And let's suppose a fellow manages to trim off twelve of those pounds. That leaves him at least three pounds heavier than he was. And suppose he repeats the pattern again—gains fifteen and loses twelve. Well, you can do the arithmetic for yourself. So the weight's creeping up, and in five or six years he's really overweight. I'm lucky; I can eat almost anything I want to—for example, I love seafood—but I don't eat bread.

Chances are you don't have a weight problem at your age, but you should go easy on the sweets and the starches, which add calories. And, in general, watch out for all that junk that scores a hit with your sweet tooth but strikes out nutritionally. Eat the foods that not only are going to give you energy but build your muscles and benefit your eyesight.

No Bad Habits

Part of staying in condition is as much *not* doing certain things as it is doing others. For instance, I've known a lot of ballplayers who drink themselves right out of the big leagues. I never drank anything alcoholic until I was nineteen, when I became a major-leaguer and had my first drink of beer. At that time you had to be twenty-one to go to a bar or buy beer, so I had to drink mine in the clubhouse. But not drinking didn't bother me. Now, as an adult, I may have a beer or a cocktail, but seldom more than one, and never before a game. You've heard the expression that drinking and driving don't mix. Well, neither do drinking and hitting. Alcohol deadens your reflexes and dulls your quickness. Anything that does those things should be avoided.

For anyone serious about athletics, narcotics are definitely a no-no. I have never seen a ballplayer who can stimulate himself by smoking or similar habits. I don't think any youngster should feel he can do himself or his team any good by smoking.

Rest

Any ballplayer can tell you what the wear-and-tear of jet travel and the long season does to his abilities. Just playing the game hard is tiring. Major-leaguers rest as much as they can, and so should you. Make sure you get enough sleep.

Legs

The legs are very, very important in baseball, and so one thing I make sure to do is run all winter. I'm a member of the YMCA, which has very good facilities, and every day I get a chance, I run in the gym. I also play volleyball and I've taken karate lessons—not for self-defense, but to help my legs.

I begin going to the gym about two weeks after the season is over. The reason I don't start directly after the season is that I like to take a little vacation, relax a bit and get my mind kind of geared to the winter months. When I first start going to the gym I'll run half a mile, then a mile, and close to the beginning of the next season I'll be running about two-and-a-half miles, so my legs will be in pretty good shape. When I get to spring training I haven't seen the ball yet, but I can run as many laps as the pitchers can, and they've started training several weeks earlier.

Before a game it's a good idea to stretch your legs to loosen them before you start running—you'll see major-leaguers do this—because you're bound to experience a situation when you're going to have to break real quick and you don't want to risk a pulled muscle. That sudden start might be called for even if the ball isn't hit right at you but in your general direction. I've never had a pulled muscle since I've been playing professional baseball. Even when I don't take infield practice before a game, I still make sure that I stretch my legs real well in the clubhouse.

Some disabilities are unavoidable. I've had fluid in my right knee, for instance, and it's painful, and I'd get weak and tired late in a game, especially in those that ran into extra innings. But, in general, good conditioning will lessen the chance of painful injuries.

Stay Warm

In certain cities and particularly at night, you'll run into chilly weather. Take care to warm up gradually. I know I'm cautious enough to take enough time to warm up in cool cities like San Francisco.

Muscle Development

For a short time when I was a kid I worked as an iceman, lugging fifty-pound blocks of ice on my back up a couple of flights of stairs. This is one way to develop muscles, but it's exhausting work and there aren't many iceman jobs around nowadays.

A lot of people think that weights are the best device for building muscles, but there are things to look out for in connection with them. You don't want to be heavy in the legs because then you're more likely to have pulled muscles and problems of this sort. Harmon "Killer" Killebrew has had a lot of problems with his legs because he's so muscular there. So you don't want to overdo the muscle development.

I'll lift weights only with my legs because I want to get them strong in spring training. I don't use them over the winter. And I don't lift weights otherwise because I really don't know how to do it. I won't let my sixteen-year-old son who plays football get on a weight program unless he's properly supervised because, while lifting weights can be very good, it can hurt you too if you don't know the right way to do it.

Joe Rudi of the Oakland A's credits a weightlifting program with considerably improving his hitting and making him quicker in the outfield, but he's done his lifting with a friend who's an expert in it.

So be sure to get proper supervision before you do any weightlifting.

Wrist Development

People often refer to my "great" wrists. As I mentioned before, they're a God-given blessing, but I've always worked to improve on my natural gifts. Once I knew that baseball was going to be my livelihood, I realized how important it was for me to work on strengthening my wrists. I used to squeeze little rubber balls and do other things to exercise my wrists. Squeezing a rubber ball is a great way to develop *your* wrists. Anything that will help make your hands strong and quick is good. What's nice about using a rubber ball is that you can do other things at the same time—like watch television or read a book.

There are other ways of strengthening your wrists, too. Bud Harrelson of the Mets used to use a homemade device consisting of a stick with a ten-pound weight at the bottom of it. He'd roll it up with his wrists and then down. He found his arms got tired very quickly, but he notes he could almost feel the strength building, not only in his wrists but in his hands and forearms as well. He also suggests doubling up a towel, and with your wrists working in opposite directions, twisting it one way, then the other. Some players recommend doing fingertip push-ups or swinging heavy bats.

Incidentally, the only baseball activity I do in the off-season is swing a bat. I try to do that about three days a week—maybe fifty times in the course of a day.

"I try to concentrate as hard in the batting cage as I do when I'm up at bat in the game. Batting practice is an ideal time to work on your hitting weaknesses."

Other Sports

Especially if you live in a climate where you can't play baseball all year, participating in other sports will help you with baseball. Some help more than others. One sport that I would particularly recommend is handball. I've found while in the major leagues that playing handball gave me good coordination and helped develop me around the chest. And it made me wider and stronger. I didn't do anything as a youngster to develop myself in this way, but it's to your advantage to participate when you're young.

Basketball is another good activity to help you sharpen the basic qualities that go into good baseball development. Handball is probably the best of all, but I would recommend almost any sport that keeps you in shape, makes you stronger and develops you quicker.

POP-TOPS TO HORSEHIDE—PRACTICE, PRACTICE

106

When I was a boy in Mobile, I used to walk along the street hitting all sorts of things with a bat or a broomstick—tin cans, even soda-pop tops when I had nothing else to hit. Either another kid would throw to me or I'd hit out of my hand.

One way or another, it was practice, which is something you can't get enough of. It may not make you perfect, but it sure will improve your hitting—if you go about it the right way.

Sometimes we'd do our pop-top hitting under the street lights in a game that had boundaries marked out for singles, extra-base hits, etc. Today, of course, you're not limited to the streets or broomsticks or pop-tops; you can practice safely on a baseball field with good equipment.

Never Too Much

If you think you've reached a point (so good or so bad) where practice can't help you anymore, just keep this in mind: You might expect that after, say, 100 games, all we major-league baseball players have to do is come out and play the game, but we don't. It's important for you Little-Leaguers, and others, to realize that as much as we practice in spring training, and as much as we play the actual games, we professionals still take batting practice before 162 games a regular season! And the smart ballplayer takes full advantage of the opportunity to improve.

A couple of Oakland A's decided to skip batting practice before the seventh game of the 1973 World Series, which they won. But keep in mind they were exceptions, it was after a whole season plus playoffs and six Series games, and they were trying to break out of a hitting slump.

Practice is an unending thing. Ted Williams claimed he used to practice until his blisters bled, and I believe him. Follow the example of great hitters and work to get better.

Swing Down

As I mentioned in the section about swinging, there's one thing you can do that can't help but improve your swing, and that's to swing *down* on the ball. Just as if you're taking an ax and chopping wood, take a bat and swing down.

If you practice swinging down on the ball, you'll be keeping your eye on it. When you swing down, everything naturally goes with you, and your concentration, your head and everything else just follows the baseball. But if you're swinging up at the ball, you've got to look up, and the first thing you know is that your head's going up. So practice swinging down just as if you're chopping a log with an ax.

107

Work on Your Weakness

I really can't blame you if you go into the batting cage and try to make yourself look good and feel good by hitting waist-high fastballs or whatever type of pitch you know you can handle. But that's not going to help you where you need help the most—learning to hit pitches you have trouble with.

What you should do is work on your weakness, and this applies whether you're hoping to play professional ball or just planning to stay in amateur ball. If you're having trouble hitting a slider, ask whoever is throwing batting practice that particular day to throw you sliders. Or if curves are your enemy, tell him to throw curves. Enough practice can turn your weakness into strength.

I was helped a lot by Mickey Owen, a former Brooklyn Dodger catcher who was my manager in the Puerto Rican League in the winter of 1953. When I was a young ballplayer I was a dead pull hitter, but he helped me change. Although I was hitting over .300 as a pull hitter, he used to take me out to the ballpark with buckets of baseballs and for hours have me hit ten to right, ten to left and maybe thirty down the middle. This made me capable of hitting to all fields, and even though in recent seasons I've gone back almost exclusively to pull hitting, it certainly helped me stay in the big leagues.

It seems today players don't get into the batting cage often enough or for long enough periods of time. If you're in a league where the emphasis is on playing games instead of practicing, you're probably not going to get enough time in the batting cage. In any case, you should make the most of the time you do get to spend there.

Unfortunately, a lot of ballplayers go in there and may hit two or three balls well and they're satisfied. But what they—and you—should do is go in that cage and keep at it as long as the team's schedule permits.

Again, I emphasize that you don't concentrate on what you already do best. I can go into the cage and probably hit ten out of a dozen pitches out of the ballpark, but that won't accomplish anything for me in the game. Instead, I use batting practice to sharpen my concentration, to make sure I'm keeping my eye on the ball and that I can give some direction to it.

Weighted Bat

It's a good idea, even before you take batting practice, to swing a weighted bat. Swinging a bat that's weighted with a donut or in some other fashion will help loosen your arms and hands, and make the bat you swing with at the plate seem lighter than it actually is. Do the same before you step in to hit during a game.

Regulation Distance

When you're practice hitting, it's definitely an advantage if the fellow throwing to you stands the regulation distance away from you, and, if possible, on a mound of regulation height so you can get used to game conditions.

But it's also helpful to practice in other ways where this isn't possible. Pepper games, in which a few players stand near a batter and quickly throw the ball to him as soon as they field the previous one, are good for sharpening reflexes. You can also practice hitting against machines that some teams own. Just swinging a bat is better than nothing. You can practice with anything, even a rubber ball that you suspend from a tree.

Reflect on Your Style

I'm not suggesting you fall in love with your batting form, but it's not a bad idea to practice swinging in front of a mirror.

About five years ago I began taking karate lessons to keep my legs in shape (something that gets more and more important as you get older) and the instructor gave me a series of things he wanted me to practice before I came back to school the next day. So I put a mirror in my basement and practiced in front of it. Then, when I had a sports show on a local television station in Atlanta, officials there told me to practice in front of a mirror. In both instances, seeing what I was doing right and wrong was helpful.

So it certainly can help you to practice in front of a mirror, but not your mother's good one. Get yourself a full-length old mirror and put it up in some safe place like your basement. If possible, get yourself an artificial plate and keep on swinging, noticing such matters as whether you're able to hit an imaginary ball over any part of the plate, and whether your swing is smooth. And stay a respectful distance away from the mirror.

Bat Speed

Concentrate on developing bat speed. Be sure you don't bring the bat back too far, but rather start from one point and get around with the bat. It's an important fundamental to practice because you'll always have pitchers in the big leagues—and probably some in the Little League, too—who can throw the ball right past you. Every split second counts, and the time wasted in recovering from a backswing can cost you contact with the ball. Practice being quick, both on the field and in front of your mirror.

Slumps

The best of hitters have slumps. I don't think there's ever been a ballplayer who hasn't. You keep reading about those fantastic batting averages in the *Red Book*—a player hitting .400, for instance. But somewhere down the line, in the course of the year, he cooled off for a period, even if the slump wasn't a serious one. Sometimes slumps vanish as mysteriously as they arrive.

Different hitters have different approaches to trying to break slumps. I don't believe in taking extra hitting practice, especially if it's midseason, because I've found that no matter how bad the slump I'm in may be, I can still hit one shot after another into the stands in batting practice. I don't think this is solving anything. The real concentration comes when you have to face that opposing pitcher who's throwing live bullets. The time you get yourself out of a slump is showdown time—when that pitcher is throwing you good curves and good fastballs, and you don't know what's coming.

If you find yourself in a slump and you want to take extra batting practice, it might be a good idea to let the man throwing batting practice surprise you, so you get used to hitting pitches you don't expect.

Never Satisfied

I don't think there was a time between the ages of twelve and seventeen when I didn't pick up a baseball bat, even in wintertime, to try to correct something, possibly to make my hands a little stronger and a lot quicker.

Even today, after twenty years in the "majors", I always feel there's room for improvement. Like if I hit two homers and a double, I wonder why I wasn't able to hit three homers. In a way, I'm never satisfied (but I also believe that in playing baseball or any sport, you can't be as good as the other guy *every* day). I've never really been satisfied with a season since I began playing the game. When you get satisfied, you get complacent.

A player at any level can improve his game, but it takes hard work. Remember Ted Williams and his blisters. Anytime you're successful at anything it means that you've worked very hard and put in some long hours. But at the end the sweat and the effort always pay off.

110

8
Mind and Heart

Baseball isn't played just on the ballfield; it's played in the players' heads and hearts. So let's talk about what may be the most important equipment a batter needs to be good—the mental and psychological equipment.

SELF-CONFIDENCE

"You've got to believe" is the motto the New York Mets, led by Tug McGraw, adopted during the 1973 season as they moved from last place in their division late in the year to first place and the National League pennant.

That motto is a good one for you. You've got to believe that you can play baseball. You've got to believe you can hit each time you get to the plate.

When Bobby Thomson hit his "home run heard 'round the world" to give the New York Giants a one-out, come-from-behind playoff win over the Brooklyn Dodgers and the 1951 National League pennant, the batter on deck was a young man named Willie Mays. Willie admitted recently that he just about prayed that the outcome of that crucial game wouldn't be left to him. Yet in the 1973 World Series, he wanted to hit at the most critical times when the pressure was heaviest. You should try to reach a point with self-confidence that you hope *you're* the one who comes up when the chips are down.

Psyching

111

In the showdown between the batter and pitcher, I would say about 75 percent of the competition is where a good hitter kind of psychs a pitcher out.

Sometimes just knowing that he's got to face a hitter like me will get a pitcher shaky, especially if he's a kid. The reverse also holds true: Sometimes a hitter will go into a series or game facing a tough pitcher and the hitter's already psyched himself out that he's going to make out.

You've got to go up to the plate with the idea that you're better than the pitcher. That's often hard to do, especially when you're facing a budding Bob Gibson or Tom Seaver, but still you've got to psych yourself into believing it. Getting base hits off him, off course, is the most convincing way.

Believe it or not, I'd rather face pitchers like Seaver or Gibson because I've got an idea of basically how they're going to pitch to me. Also, I know they're not afraid to pitch me; they're going to go out there and prove they can get me out. Because they're challenging me, I'm going to have to hit their pitching.

There's an old controversy in baseball: When a good pitcher faces a good hitter, who has the advantage? I feel it's just about half-and-half when it comes to each one's confidence and concern about his adversary. But overall, I feel the hitter definitely has the advantage because the pitcher has to throw strikes, and no matter who it is out there on the mound, he's going to have to throw a pitch to hit within the strike zone.

A little nervousness when you step to the plate is to be expected, and provided it doesn't affect your control, it isn't a bad thing. With self-confidence you'll be able to handle your nervousness. I'm not talking about *over*confidence, but rather an appreciation of what you're able to do against any pitcher, with practice and the right mental attitude.

Desire

The key to the right mental attitude is desire. Whatever you want to do in life, the desire to be the best you can has to be very intense, so strong that you're willing to accept the discipline and hard work that excellence demands. Desire is the No. 1 quality of a good hitter.

You're not always going to have good days; not even the best hitters in baseball always have them. There will be games when you go 0-for-4 and you're not going to hit the balls you think you should be hitting. But the player with desire is the one who realizes there's always another day, another game. Whether you went 0-for-4 or 4-for-4, it's history, and the important thing is to concentrate on the game you're playing *now*.

Your dedication to the game should show even before you start to

112

play. In my family we kids couldn't go out to play until we'd cut enough wood for the stove. I have to admit there were times I put some of my unchopped wood into my brother's pile so I'd get out to play sooner. But on the other hand, I'd often help friends do their chores so they could get to play sooner and we could get a ballgame started. I mention this as an evidence of really wanting to play.

Hustle

Once on the field, you've got to give your best effort at all times. Every time you hit a ball, hustle down to first. Even the steadiest of fielders will sometimes make an error, and the fact that you ran out what you hit could turn a ballgame around. If it's a base hit, hustling down the line can result in an extra base. Or you might draw a throw and allow a runner who's farther along to take an extra base and maybe even score.

I feel it's to my advantage and my team's for me to run as soon as the ball is hit. Of course, there's no sense running if you hit a foul fifteen rows back into the stands. And if you pop the ball up in the infield, you don't have to tear down the line, because the only place you can go if the fielder drops it is first base. But on a ground ball, run hard to first because there's no telling what that ball might do.

In a game against the Cubs during the '73 season I hit an infield grounder that looked like a routine out. Still I ran the ball out and the first baseman dropped the ball. Unfortunately, the ball didn't get far enough away and Ralph Garr got thrown out at home plate, but it could have been a two-base error.

Even on a walk, you should hustle down. It's rare, but I have made it to second on a ball-four pitch that got away from the catcher. And you should be alert on a third strike; if it gets away from the catcher and first base is open, you can try to make it safely to first. This happened in the 1941 World Series on a pitch that got away from Mickey Owen of the Dodgers. The hitter, Tommy Henrich, made it to first to get a rally going, and his team, the Yankees, who were behind, won the game.

I may sometimes look as if I'm running easily to first on a base hit, but I'm watching the outfielder, and if he messes up I can accelerate. I have the speed to shift gears. A major-leaguer, with customers in the stands who have paid $2.50 to $3.50 to see him play, should give his best for two-and-a-half hours. And major-leaguer or not, you owe it to *yourself* and your team to play all-out.

Pride

Another quality a player needs to be good is pride. I think you owe it to yourself, the fans who come to see you play and, in the case of professional athletes, the people you're working for to be proud of your team and the fact that you're playing organized ball.

Intelligence

For a hitter, intelligence is a very important quality. You've got to study the game constantly and concentrate all the time. You've got to be aware of the pitcher's capabilities and what he's throwing; what the game situation is; how many are out; how many are on base; who's coming up next; and what the count is.

I think if you've got a hard-headed ballplayer who can't or won't learn, doesn't pick up things quickly, he isn't going to make it in the majors, even if he has a world of talent. The less-talented player who learns quickly will get to the "majors" sooner than the more-talented one who refuses to learn and acts as if he knows everything.

LISTEN TO ADVICE

One of the most common mistakes I see young athletes make—and this applies not only to hitting, not only to baseball, but to sports in general—is that they don't listen to the advice of older players, coaches or managers. They feel that all the skills and understanding can come relatively easily to them, but this is impossible.

The only way you're going to be good, the only way you're going to be successful in sports, no matter how much talent you have, is to practice and work hard regardless of the sacrifice involved.

One particular pro football player had an awful lot of talent, but he thought he didn't have to go by the rules. But you *have* to play by the rules, no matter how much talent you enjoy. You have to be part of a team and you have to have your teammates like you.

I've been fortunate enough to play in two World Series and 21 or 22 All-Star games, and I've gotten along with everyone I've ever played with, simply because I don't want anyone to give me any special kind of privileges. Once you get to the point where you expect privileges you're going to lose the respect of your teammates and you'll defeat your own

114

purposes. This is as true on your team as it is on mine. So play by the rules, remember that you're part of a team, and listen to advice.

Everybody can learn, and your manager or coach is there to teach. Remember, he's got the experience and the overall interest of the team at heart. So take his advice and use it to advantage. Don't gripe at what he tells you or has you do. In my experience, it's usually been the "fringe" ballplayers who are involved in any friction with the manager, players looking for an excuse and somebody to blame.

EFFECT OF FIELDING ON HITTING

Everything you do, especially in the field, is going to have an effect on your hitting. If you make an error in the field or lose a ball in the lights—or whatever—the next time you're up you're likely to try extra hard to get a base hit. I know from personal experience that it's hard to resist the temptation to try to make up for the miscue in the field by extra effort at the plate. It's human nature to do this, but if possible you should try to overcome this overanxiousness, because if you're pressing too hard at the plate you're not likely to connect solidly. It all adds up to forgetting last inning's misfortune and concentrating on the pitch right now.

PSYCHOLOGY OF SLUMPS

I'm sure that the mind plays an awfully big role in slumps. As mentioned earlier, a slump is something everyone is going to go through if he plays this game for any length of time. Sometimes you worry so much about your slump that you begin pressing and worrying and end up changing your style—with the result that your slump gets worse.

So when I have a slump I try not to let it worry me. That's the No. 1 thing. Naturally it will worry me a bit—you can't just wish worry away —but it doesn't have a damaging mental effect on me. What I try to do is come out to the ballpark with the idea of erasing from my mind what happened yesterday or the day before and just concentrate on today's pitcher and what he's throwing.

Many good hitters recommend that the way to get out of a slump is swing to hit through the middle and make sure you're watching the ball. Determine that you're not going to go after bad pitches. Some suggest

115

choking up on the bat. If it works for you, fine, but as a player who once lost 62 points in his batting average in two weeks, my idea is to just go up there and swing normally. (I have on occasion resorted to a slightly heavier bat than usual.) That's usually all that's needed. I remember once in 1969 going 0 for 16. Then, against the Dodgers, I got an early-inning single and hit another safety to tie the game at 3-all. In the twelfth inning I came to the plate with the score tied at 5. The pitcher, rookie Ray Lamb, came in with three fastballs. He got by with the first two, but I hit the third into the Dodger bullpen for a 6-5 victory and we moved into first place in our division.

MY CHOICE OF HITTERS

If I see ten youngsters swinging a bat and I'm trying to decide which one is likely to develop into a major-leaguer, there are certain things I'll look for. First, when he hits the ball, I look to see whether it *jumps* off the bat. By that I mean whether it carries. This reflects a quality he's got to have to some degree: natural ability.

But natural ability is only one part, it's only the potential. What happens to that potential depends on a factor I look for next: attitude. I want to know whether he's willing to learn. If he isn't, his talent isn't going to be enough.

I've seen a lot of ballplayers with a lot of talent *abuse* what they have, and the first thing you know they're back in the minors and they don't know why. They know they're talented, but they're thirty-five years old before they realize, "Man, I could have made it earlier. But I've wasted ten years."

GO WITH WHAT YOU'VE GOT

Somebody with less natural ability but a great willingness to learn may go further in the sport. Maury Wills, who kicked around the minor leagues about a dozen years before becoming a major-league star, is a great example. He didn't have much natural ability, but he worked hard teaching himself and deciding how best to make the most of what he did best. He knew he had speed, but the problem was how to get on base so he could help some ballclub with it. When he couldn't do much hitting right-handed, he began switch-hitting. He got on base often enough to take advantage of his speed, and went on to help the Dodgers win two or three pennants, breaking Ty Cobb's stolen-base record with 104 in one season and winning the 1962 National League's Most Valuable Player award at the same time.

Maybe there's something of the Maury Wills quality in you. You don't have great natural ability, but you do have great desire, which will over-come. The importance of doing your own thing in baseball—doing what you can do best—can't be stressed enough.

Some ballplayers would comment about how Maury would sometimes steal a base when his club was leading by a lot of runs. All he was doing was taking advantage of what he had. He had to do things he knew he could do best. If I get to the plate and we're ten runs ahead, I'm certainly not going to be trying to pop up. I'm going to be trying to hit the ball, and if it goes out of the ballpark, fine. I'm not trying to show up the other ballplayers. I'm trying to do what I can do best. And Maury Wills was doing what he could do best.

So, yes, I want to know if a ballplayer is willing to learn. Everybody needs to be taught something, just as I did, when Mickey Owen had me come out and learn to hit to the opposite field. I had to be willing to make the sacrifice of getting up and out at eight in the morning while my team-mates slept. And I *was* willing, because it was a skill I had to learn, and I was fortunate to have a manager who was willing to teach me.

If you want to be successful in hitting, or for that matter in any other aspect of any other sport, you've got to be willing to sacrifice. You may be rapping the ball at a .350 clip, but if the team is out on the field early in the morning, you've got to be out there too. And you've got to work hard to show that you want to learn and that you want to be part of the team.

I look at all this—at a youngster's attitude; at how his teammates regard him; whether he's a team player or a selfish player. I want to know whether you can teach him anything, because, as we've said, if he has the natural ability and you're not able to talk to him, you're not going to be able to teach him anything and his development as a player is going to be limited.

When you have it fixed in your mind that you want to work hard, that you want to be part of a team, that you want to learn—and you've got some ability—you're on your way to becoming a terrific ballplayer.

Nobody likes to lose—I know I don't. Defeat is a hard pill to swallow.

No matter what you play—baseball, football, basketball, soccer, or what have you—no matter who you are and how good you are, you're going to run into someone who's going to beat you, some teams that are going to beat you, and you're going to run into some seasons that are losers. You've got to be able to cope. Throwing a bat or kicking a locker doesn't do a thing for your batting average.

Your coach can do you no greater favor than to teach you the fundamentals of the game and point out that losing is a part of playing. Unfortunately, in some organized leagues—at least on some of the teams—there's too much emphasis on "we've got to win" and not enough on fundamentals. If you've mastered your fundamentals and given your best, you should be able to take victory or defeat without losing your head.

Be grateful for the coach or manager who instructs you in the basics and teaches you how to win but who knows that winning isn't everything. Baseball should be a lot of fun, and trying your best to win is part of that enjoyment, but too much emphasis on winning can take the fun out of it. That's why some coaches are criticized for teaching boys to throw breaking balls before they're old enough. At your age you're still developing. Your arm is growing and getting stronger, and the only thing you should concentrate on is throwing strikes. When you're twenty years old you can concentrate on the breaking ball. But do it too soon and you run the risk of a sore arm that could put a halt to your baseball career before it begins.

So by all means, play in Little League and Pony League and Babe Ruth League and all the rest, but don't ever forget that baseball is a *game*.

Getting Angry

There are bound to be times when you're angry, usually at yourself. Things also bother me, but I react differently than other people. Some guys go 0-for-4 and throw their helmets or kick things, but I think, "Why did I pop up? Why did I strike out?" This is how I try to teach my own children—to sit down and figure it out.

And this is what I recommend to you. Figure out what you do best. Figure out what needs improving. Then work as hard as you can on overcoming your weaknesses and capitalizing on your strengths. Hustle, observe, think—and practice, practice, practice. Make yourself the best ballplayer you can be.

118

Showdown Revisited

So there you are at the plate in the bottom of the ninth with a man on second, two outs and your team trailing by a run. Waiting on deck, you watched the pitcher and noticed that his fastball, instead of rising a little as it crossed the plate, the way it had earlier in the game, was now hanging a bit.

You'd been having trouble with outside fastballs the last few games, and so you worked on that weakness in batting practice. But that was practice; this is the real thing. You want very badly to come through in the clutch, especially because of that error you made last inning in overrunning a ground single and letting the runners advance. But, as your coach reminded you—and he knows you so well—you don't want to let an error in the field make you overanxious at the plate. You're going to wait for a good pitch in the strike zone to hit.

You look down to your third-base coach for a sign, even though you know what you have to do. You take the donut off your relatively light bat, adjust your helmet and step in. You hope the pitcher is convinced by your stance and appearance that you're confident you can hit him, even though he's retired you in your last three trips to the plate. You particularly remember the change-up he fooled you with to strike you out.

Standing back in the box where you're comfortable with a slightly open stance, your legs spread moderately apart, your weight evenly balanced, you make sure your bat can hit a ball over any part of the plate.

The pitcher winds and throws. You stride but keep your bat back so that if it's a change-up you'll have some power left to hit it. The pitch *is* a change-up, but it's far outside. Ball one.

You take a deep breath. It's been an exhausting, tense game. Luckily, you're in good shape and you had a good night's sleep. You need all the concentration and energy you can muster.

Again the pitcher goes into his motion. You consider faking a bunt to get the first and third basemen moving in, but you decide it's too much wasted effort. They're probably not going to be fooled, and anyway you need complete concentration on hitting the ball.

Another change comes in. You swing a little too soon and foul it off. The count is 1-and-1.

The tension is mounting. When the pitcher delays, you ask the umpire to call time and step out of the box. You again remind yourself that earlier in the game the pitcher struck you out on a change. Will he come in with still another one? Or will he go to his fastball? You've got to be ready for either one.

Once more the pitcher goes into his motion. Watching the ball from the moment it leaves his hand, you pivot your hips backward. Your weight shifts slightly to the back foot as you stride with your front foot into the pitch—a fastball high and toward the outside corner of the plate. It's letter-high in the strike zone. If it rises, it could give you trouble, but if it hangs—as you noticed it doing the last few innings—you should be able to give it a good ride.

You swing—but not for the seats and not from the heels, which would increase the possibility of missing the ball. Rather, it's a strong swing intended to meet the ball solidly for a base hit. You want to make contact with the ball in front of the plate. You pivot your hips forward, your weight shifting to your front foot. The ball hangs for an instant and you whip the bat into the ball with your shoulders, arms and wrists. Your swing is downward, smooth and in a wide arc, heading for an arms-extended follow-through. Your head is down. Crash! All the elements come together. Your bat meets the ball solidly and propels it hard, even though you're not usually a power hitter. You hustle to first and catch a glimpse of the ball. It's taken off to right-center field, rising on a line toward the fence. It's a two-run homer and you've won the game!

* * *

Fantasy? Yes. But certainly possible if you put it all together.
Go to it, and best of luck.

Here I am with Darrell Evans (left) and Davey Johnson on September 30th, 1973—the day I hit my 40th home run of the season—the first time three ball players on one club hit 40 or more home runs in a season. They both hit more than I did, with Darrell slamming 41 and Davey 43—that figure being more home runs than any second baseman ever hit before.

HANK AARON'S
RECORD BOOK

National League Records:

    Most years with 40 or more home runs, eight.
    Most years with 600 or more at bats, ten.
    Most years with 30 or more homers, 15.
    Most years with one or more homers in all parks, nine.
    Most years with 100 or more RBI, 11.
    Most years with 100 or more runs scored, 15.
    Most years leading league in total bases, eight.
    Most years with 300 or more total bases, 15.
    Most years playing in 150 or more games, 14.
    Most years with 100 or more extra bases on long hits, 19.
    Most consecutive years with 100 or more runs scored, 13.
    Most years with 20 or more homers, 19.
    Most consecutive years with 20 or more homers, 19.
    Most career total bases, 6,424.
    Most career sacrifice flies, 111.
    Most career intentional walks, 283.
    Most career home runs, 713.
    Most career RBI, 2,133.
    Most career extra base hits, 1,393.

National League Records Tied:

Most grand slam home runs, 14 with W. McCovey and G. Hodges.
Most walks in one game, 5 with many.
Most years leading the league in RBI, 4 with R. Hornsby.

Major League Records:

Most years with 100 or more runs scored, 15.
Most years leading league in total bases, 8.
Most years with 300 or more total bases, 15.
Most years playing in 150 or more games, 14.
Most years 100 or more extra bases on long hits, 19.
Most career total bases, 6,424.
Most career extra base hits, 1,393.
Most years with 30 or more homers, 15.
Most years with 20 or more homers, 19.
Most consecutive years with 20 or more homers, 19.
Most career sacrifice flies, 111.
Most career intentional walks, 283.
Most home runs in one league, 713.

Major League Records Tied:

Most consecutive years with 100 or more runs, 13 with Lou Gehrig.

BATTING RECORD

Bold face figures indicate led league or tied for league lead.

Year Club	League	G	AB	R	H	TB	2B	3B	HR	RBI	SB	Pct.
1952 Eau Claire	Northern	87	345	79	116	170	19	4	9	61	25	.336
1953 Jacksonville	So. Atlantic	137	574	**115**	**208**	**338**	36	14	22	**125**	13	.362
1954 Milwaukee	National	122	468	58	131	209	27	6	13	69	2	.280
1955 Milwaukee	National	153	602	105	189	325	37	9	27	106	3	.314
1956 Milwaukee	National	153	609	106	**200**	**340**	34	14	26	92	2	.328
1957 Milwaukee	National	151	615	**118**	198	**369**	27	6	**44**	**132**	1	.322
1958 Milwaukee	National	153	601	109	196	328	34	4	30	95	4	.326
1959 Milwaukee	National	154	629	116	**223**	**400**	46	7	39	123	8	**.355**
1960 Milwaukee	National	153	590	102	172	**334**	20	11	40	**126**	16	.292
1961 Milwaukee	National	155	603	115	197	**358**	39	10	34	120	21	.327
1962 Milwaukee	National	156	592	127	191	366	28	6	45	128	15	.323
1963 Milwaukee	National	161	631	**121**	201	**370**	29	4	**44**	**130**	31	.319
1964 Milwaukee	National	145	570	103	187	293	30	2	24	95	22	.328
1965 Milwaukee	National	150	570	109	181	319	40	1	32	89	24	.318
1966 Atlanta	National	158	603	117	168	325	23	1	**44**	**127**	21	.279
1967 Atlanta	National	155	600	**113**	184	**344**	37	3	**39**	109	17	.307
1968 Atlanta	National	160	606	84	174	302	33	4	29	86	28	.287
1969 Atlanta	National	147	547	100	164	**332**	30	3	44	97	9	.300
1970 Atlanta	National	150	516	103	154	296	26	1	38	118	9	.298
1971 Atlanta	National	139	495	95	162	331	22	3	47	118	1	.327
1972 Atlanta	National	129	449	75	119	231	10	0	34	77	4	.265
1973 Atlanta	National	120	392	84	118	252	12	1	40	96	1	.301
Major League Totals	20 Years	2964	11288	2060	3509	6424	584	96	713	2133	239	.311

WORLD SERIES RECORD

Year Club	League	G	AB	R	H	TB	2B	3B	HR	RBI	SB	Pct.
1957 Milwaukee vs New York		7	28	5	11	22	0	1	3	7	0	.393
1958 Milwaukee vs New York		7	27	3	9	11	2	0	0	2	0	.333
World Series Totals		14	55	8	20	33	2	1	3	9	0	.364

CHAMPIONSHIP SERIES RECORD

Year Club	League	G	AB	R	H	TB	2B	3B	HR	RBI	SB	Pct.
1969 Atlanta vs New York		3	14	3	5	16	2	0	3	7	0	.357

ALL-STAR GAME RECORD

Year Club	League	G	AB	R	H	TB	2B	3B	HR	RBI	SB	Pct.
1955 at Milwaukee	rf	2	1	2	2	0	0	0	1	0	1.000	
1956 at Washington	lf	1	0	0	0	0	0	0	0	0	.000	
1957 at St. Louis	rf	4	0	1	1	0	0	0	0	0	.250	
1958 at Baltimore	rf	2	0	0	0	0	0	0	1	0	.000	
1959 at Pittsburgh	rf	4	1	2	0	0	0	0	1	0	.500	
at Los Angeles	rf	3	0	0	0	0	0	0	1	0	.000	
1960 at Kansas City	rf	4	0	0	0	0	0	0	0	0	.000	
at New York (American)	rf	3	0	0	0	0	0	0	0	0	.000	
1961 at San Francisco	ph	1	1	1	1	0	0	0	0	0	1.000	
at Boston	rf	2	0	0	0	0	0	0	0	0	.000	
1962 at Chicago (National)	cf	2	0	0	0	0	0	0	0	0	.000	
1963 at Cleveland	rf	4	1	0	0	0	0	0	0	0	.000	
1964 at New York (National)	ph	1	0	0	0	0	0	0	0	0	.000	
1965 at Minnesota	rf	5	0	1	1	0	0	0	0	0	.200	
1966 at St. Louis	lf	4	0	0	0	0	0	0	0	0	.000	
1967 at California	cf-lf	6	0	1	1	0	0	0	0	1	.167	
1968 at Houston	rf	3	0	1	1	0	0	0	0	1	.333	
1969 at Washington	rf	4	1	1	1	0	0	0	0	0	.250	
1970 at Cincinnati	rf	2	0	0	0	0	0	0	0	0	.000	
1971 at Detroit	rf	2	1	1	4	0	0	1	1	0	.500	
1972 at Atlanta	rf	3	1	1	4	0	0	1	2	0	.333	
1973 at Kansas City	1b	2	0	1	1	0	0	0	1	0	.500	
All-Star Game Totals	22	64	7	13	17	0	0	2	8	2	.203	

Member of National League All-Star team in 1962 (first game), did not play, ankle injury.

125

The Babe and me.

AARON vs. RUTH

	Yrs.	G	AB	R	H	TB	1B	2B	3B	HR	RBI	EBH	SB	Pct.	SA
aron	20	2964	11288	2060	3509	6424	2116	584	96	713	2133	1393	239	.311	.569
uth	22	2503	8399	2174	2873	5793	1517	506	136	714	2209	1356	123	.342	.690

Here is how Aaron stood in the major lifetime hitting categories at the end of the 1973 baseball season.

Games—Cobb 3,033; Musial 3,026; Mays 2,992; AARON 2,964.

At Bat—Cobb 11,429; AARON 11,288.

Runs—Cobb 2,244; Ruth, 2,174; Mays 2,062; AARON 2,060.

Hits—Cobb 4,191; Musial 3,630; Speaker 3,515; AARON 3,509.

Total Bases—AARON 6,424.

Home Runs—Ruth 714; AARON 713.

Runs Batted In—Ruth 2,209; AARON 2,133.

Extra Base Hits—AARON 1,393.

Doubles—Speaker 793; Musial 725; Cobb 724; Wagner 651; Lajoie 650; Waner 603; AARON 584.

Two or More Homers in One Game (Times Accomplished)—Ruth 72; Mays 63; AARON 61.